THE SPIRAL SHELL

Cover and Interior Design: Jordan Wannemacher

Author Photo: Sharona Jacobs

The Publisher gratefully acknowledges the following for permissions to reprint: *Promise at Dawn*, copyright ©1961 by Romain Gary. Reprinted by permission of New Directions Publishing Corp.

Parts of this book have been previously published in different form in the following: "Hiding," *ASCENT*, August 2012; "Houses," *ASCENT*, Winter 2014; *The Woven Tale Press Magazine*, February 2019; "Pilgrimage," *Ploughshares*, Winter 2014; "Hidden Messages," *Stone Voices*, Winter 2014; "The Memory Palate,1966", *A Journal of Creative Nonfiction*, Winter, 2014; "Brown Leather Satchel," *Fourth Genre*, Fall 2017;"Beautiful Hair," *Solstice: A Magazine of Diverse Voices*, Winter 2017-18

Printed in the United States

Library of Congress Control Number:2019956372.

ISBN: 9781639640027

Hardcover ISBN: 97819431561924

E-book ISBN: 9781943156931

The
SPIRAL
SHELL

A FRENCH VILLAGE REVEAL ITS SECRETS OF JEWISH RESISTANCE IN WORLD WAR II

A MEMOIR

SANDELL MORSE

Schaffner Press

For Dick

PART I

1

I knew so little of my own history. On my father's side, I had two names: Henriette Ducas and Jacques Hirsch, my great-great grand-parents, both born in Héricourt, France, a commune in the Alsace that used to go back and forth between France and Germany, a spoil of war. Newly married, the couple sailed into New York Harbor, and as far as the family knew they washed up onto American shores without a past. My father told me only those names, no names of their parents, grandparents, sisters or brothers. No stories of a family's joys or its heartbreaks and struggles. Whatever had gone before evaporated into the air of a brand-new world.

My father told me stories of his family's American successes — a brownstone on the Upper East Side, a shoe store on Fifth Avenue. "A block long," he would say, the space between his gesturing hands growing wider and wider. For me, a child given to fantasy and fairy tales, that shoe store grew into a department store, and the brownstone became a castle. Yet, there was truth to my father's stories. I had a news-paper clipping dated 1902, probably from the society pages of the *Hart-ford Courant*, announcing a marriage and listing the elegant wedding presents received, "among them being a check of a large amount from Leo M. Hirsch, an uncle of the groom." This was my great-grandfather, proprietor of that block-long shoe store.

The Hirsches were German Jews, Reform Jews, aspiring to both social status and wealth, assimilation their goal. My father taught me that being Jewish was no different from being Christian. "It's a religion, that's all," he would say, as if to convince himself as well. He wanted to pass, and he wanted me to pass. Not inside the house or among fellow Jews, but in the Christian world. He insisted Hirsch was a German, not a Jewish name.

For years, I didn't know he was wrong about our name, but I did know he was wrong about Judaism and Christianity. Growing up, I shared things with my Jewish friends I didn't share with my gentile friends — a nod, a glance, a meaningful touch on a shoulder. I knew, too, there were places I wasn't welcome. Once, visiting Grandma Rose, my father's mother, and Harry, my step-grandfather, in Miami Beach where they spent winters, I saw a sign in a window of a boarding house: No Jews. I saw signs over drinking fountains: Colored; White. With or without signs, America named its outsiders.

In that old newspaper clipping the word reverend replaced rabbi. Temple replaced synagogue. "The ceremony was performed by the Rev. Mr. Levy of the Orange Street Temple." When you changed rabbi to reverend, you tossed away centuries of learning, letting assimilation subsume knowledge and culture.

When I was a child, school forms asked for my religion. "Write Hebrew," my father would say.

"What's wrong with putting Jewish?"

"Just do it."

My friends didn't go around calling themselves Hebrews. We were Jewish (we didn't say Jew, an insult), and because we were growing up in the shadow of the Second World War, we knew about concentration camps, gas chambers, and lamp shades made of human skin. We whispered about those lamp shades on the playground the way we whispered about sex, knowing and not knowing, believing and not believing.

⁓

We moved a lot when I was a kid, New Jersey to Florida, Florida back to New Jersey. My father's heart wasn't good, and his doctor warned that if he didn't move to a warm climate, it might give out. He had reason to worry. When my father was thirteen, Sandal, his father and my namesake, rolled off a couch and died of a massive heart attack in front of his eyes. This was my father's story. Years later, my aunt, said to me, "Bullshit. He wasn't there. He was at the Shore with Rose."

I never confronted my father with my aunt's story. I was in my mid-fifties when she told me, and I understood the truth of what had happened didn't matter. The story of seeing his father die had already shaped my father's life and mine. My father longed for what might have been, and I longed for a father who knew how to love me.

After his father's funeral, my father skipped school for days, then intermittently. The truant officer brought him back. In high school, he played high-stakes poker, hung out in bars, and shot pool. He dropped out of college. He bet on the horses. "I wanted to be a dentist like my father," he said to me. "Then, my father died."

He wandered from job to job, business to business. "He can't help it," my mother said when I protested our many moves. "You have to remember how young he was when he lost his father."

"Yeah," I said. "Like he was the only person in the world who lost a father."

"Sandy," she said, admonishing me.

I flared my nostrils and curled my upper lip.

In one stint in Florida we lived in Oak Hill, a rural town with orange groves, a packing house, a general store, and a Baptist church. There

11

were eight of us in the fifth grade, and we shared a room with the sixth. Kids in my class had never seen a Jew, and when Little Jimmy called me a dirty Jew, I bloodied his nose. At home, my father didn't know whether to praise me or punish me. I gave him my sweet-girl look, big helpless eyes, sugary smile. He burst out laughing.

By the time we settled in Millburn, New Jersey, and I entered the seventh grade, I'd attended five different grammar schools. At recess I hung back and lingered at the edges. Wordlessly, I watched girls jump rope or play hopscotch. I wanted to join in, but I was afraid of being pushy. Pushy was Jewish. At home, my mother told me to remember I was Jewish. She wanted me to recognize this fact as a point of pride. My father, on the other hand, told me to look and act like the Christian girls, which was easy because I had light brown hair and blue-green eyes. I was small-boned and fine-featured. I was skinny and I ran fast. If there were Jewish kids in my class — and I knew how to figure that out — I avoided them. I could pass, until the inevitable happened. Somebody would make an anti-Semitic remark and I would have no choice. I revealed my identity.

One day, I was standing in line in the cafeteria, talking to Shirley, a popular girl in my class. She invited me over for Saturday. "We can work on our geography project," she said.

I was stunned by the invitation. At the same time, Linda who was just in front of us in line, jostled and elbowed the girl beside her. She yelled, "You're cutting! You can't cut." She backed into me, and my tray fell out of my hand and clattered on the floor. Linda, with dark curly hair and thick dark eyebrows, wore a gold Jewish star around her neck.

As I picked up my tray, Shirley whispered, "She's such a Jew." I felt queasy as if I'd tasted sour milk.

"I'm Jewish, you know," I said.

"You're not," Shirley said. "You can't be."

"I am."

"Stop kidding me."

"I'm not."

The next day, Shirley said her mother was too busy on Saturday to have me come over.

❧

When I was thirteen, I begged my father to join the synagogue. "All of my friends go," I said. "Why can't I?"

He banged a salt shaker on the kitchen table. Spicy, our black-and-white cocker spaniel, lay curled beside his chair. "Jesus, Lil, why can't you fix this thing?" he said to my mother.

She held out her hand for the shaker. "Give it to me, Leon. I'll loosen it for you."

"Never mind," he said, unscrewing the top and running his knife along the inside.

I stabbed a piece of meat with my fork. "I want to go to religious school," I said. "What's wrong with that?"

My father sipped his orange soda, paused, then sipped again.

"Leon," Mom said. "Maybe she has a point."

Mama and Papa, my mother's parents, were Orthodox. My mother rejected their Orthodoxy, but not their sensibility or identity. Justice and kindness mattered. Being Jewish mattered.

My father pointed his knife at my mother. "When I want your opinion, I'll ask for it." Ice crackled inside our glasses.

Now he aimed his knife at me. "Eat," he said. "You're not leaving this table until you finish what's on your plate." He glared at my mother and spoke in an exaggerated tone, as if he were an actor on a stage. "You haven't asked me about my day."

"I was with you, Leon," she said.

They worked together in his camera store, although my father

13

didn't call what my mother did work, selling greeting cards, film and flashbulbs, taking inventory, dusting, vacuuming, and standing at the cash register processing customers' payments. My father called that "helping out."

I was keeping my head down under the line of fire, when suddenly my father stared at my plate. "Get rid of that disgusting stuff."

I hated steak. I plucked the gray glob I had been chewing from my mouth, and set it on the side of my plate.

"Here," Mom said, "I'll take it." She took the plate and scraped the mess into a garbage pail under the sink.

Spittle formed at the corners of my father's lips. He eyed my mother. "I don't see why you let her get away with that crap."

"Maybe if I went to Hebrew school, I'd learn better manners," I shouted.

My friend Carol was studying for her bat mitzvah, and I wanted one, too.

"Look," my father said, "if I told you once, I told you a thousand times. The answer is no, Sandy, so stop beating a dead horse."

That expression made me crazy. I saw a horse, a real horse, lying in dirt, flank heaving, eyes rolling back into his head as the tail of a whip came down.

I shouted back, "You went to Sunday school. You were confirmed."

My father pulled his chair closer to the table. The legs scraped. My mother lowered her gaze. "That's the point," my father said. "Confirmation, not bar mitzvah. I've told you. We're Reformed, not Conservative. None of that mumbo jumbo."

Mumbo jumbo meant Hebrew. I narrowed my eyes and glared at my father. "You said bar mitzvah. It's bat mitzvah, with a 't'."

"I don't give a damn what it is, you're not going." He slammed his fist on the table, and his glass trembled; soda spilled. "For God's sake, Sandy, don't you ever give up? Now, see what you made me do."

14

I gripped the seat of my chair and tried hard not to bolt. I wanted to tell my father why I needed to go to Hebrew school, but I couldn't find words. That was the year Mama, my maternal grandmother died, and Papa, my grandfather, had gone to stay with Uncle Gabe and Aunt Bernice. All of my life, Mama and Papa had lived with us, enduring each of my father's many moves. Now, I came home to an empty house. At supper it was just Mom, Dad, and me. I missed Mama and Papa, terribly. Maybe if I learned the prayers Mama used to recite on *Shabbos*, her thick fingers circling the candle flames, I could bring her back.

Until I was five, we all lived together in Mama's and Papa's yellow stucco house. Afternoons, after she finished cooking, dusting, vacuuming, and hanging clothes on a line, Mama would sit at the kitchen table with her friends, Mrs. Klein and Mrs. Bodkin, all from a place they called Russ-Poland, all speaking Yiddish. I would sit on the floor at Mama's feet, dressing my paper dolls — Dagwood, Blondie and Cookie — and soaking up language. I learned about Kermit, Mrs. Bodkin's son who was "carrying on" with a *shiksa*. "God forbid he marries her." (He did. For years, Mrs. Botkin did not speak to her son. She never spoke to the *shiksa*.)

I learned from them that because my Uncle Harry had flat feet, the Army sent him home, *"Kenahora,"* *Kenahora*, a verbal equivalent of the red ribbon Mama used to pin to my undershirt every day before I left for Kindergarten. The evil eye did not like the color red.

These women of my childhood had all escaped one form of oppression or another — poverty, confinement, restrictions, pogroms. They lived, when young, in tenements on the Lower East Side. Probably, like Mama, they took in piecework.

Fridays in the yellow stucco house, the kitchen filled with the smells of *Shabbos:* chicken soup, a first-cut brisket, potato kugel, a bowl of applesauce sprinkled with cinnamon. In the dining room the table was set with a white damask cloth, cloth napkins, and our best silverware

— although it wasn't real silver — and our best dishes for *fleishig*, meat. My seat was next to Mama's, but she didn't sit. She stood, her wavy white hair covered with a black lace shawl. In front of her, two shiny brass candlesticks held white candles. She struck the tip, and a match burst into flame. A hush fell over the table. Everybody watched as Mama drew the light of *shabbos* to her heart, closed her eyes and chanted the blessing, her thin soprano sinking into my bones.

I lifted my spoon. Mama's chicken soup was golden with glistening droplets of fat skimming the surface. Mandelen and flakes of parsley floated at the surface. Mama bought her chickens live from the chicken man, who killed them in a yard out back. She cooked them in a big pot, feet floating. She said the feet gave the soup its golden color.

I breathed in the savory aroma.

At the kitchen table, the argument continued, my mother saying, "It's new, Leon, a bat mitzvah, so that girls can have the same as boys."

My father jutted his chin and stared at her with beady eyes. She swallowed air. She figured if I wanted a Jewish education, I should have one, but I knew she wouldn't fight for me, really fight. I took a breath. "I know why you won't join."

"Oh, you do, do you?" said my father. "Okay, smarty pants, tell me."

"You don't want to spend the money."

Dad leaned his body across the table, grabbed my wrist, and held on. "For your information, I can buy and sell half that congregation, so don't start with me."

My nostrils flared, and I pulled free. "I've already started."

I raced upstairs to my bedroom, slammed the door and stayed there. Later that night as I lay in bed and listened to my father's footsteps climb the stairs, I understood I would not have a bat mitzvah.

I would not learn the prayers Mama used to chant. I turned off my light and lay on my bed in the dark. A car's headlamps illuminated the ballerinas dancing on my walls, their pink tutus and pink slippers, wallpaper I'd chosen myself. I watched them move and cut through the air as if propelled by something invisible inside them. I was like those dancers. There was that something inside of me, something elusive my father could not take from me —— Mama's gift: my deep love for Judaism's soulful heart.

2

I was feeling light, buoyant, as I opened a low gate and stepped out on the sidewalk. I wore sandals, a khaki skirt, and a black tank top, silk because I'd packed light and silk rolled and snuggled into crevices. The sky was wide, and the sun's rays gave the landscape a painterly glow. Auvillar, this village, was west of Van Gogh territory, but it was nearly as far south. I imagined the light was similar.

At age seventy-one, I'd been awarded a writing residency at Moulin à Nef, an artists' retreat owned and operated by the Virginia Center for the Creative Arts (VCCA). I'd attended retreats, even for a month at a time, but had never visited a foreign country alone, never left home with the Atlantic separating Dick, my husband of more than fifty years, and me.

I hadn't expected to get in. "You have to go," Dick said.

After all these years, there were many ways to forge a marriage. Over the years, Dick may have wanted a more traditional wife, and often, I think he did, but he held onto our marriage with an open palm. A year earlier, I'd completed a memoir about my father and ultimately put it in a cupboard with other unpublished manuscripts. Inside, I imagined my characters walking and talking like puppets: Joanna, a discontented suburban housewife, protagonist of my novella—whose husband flaunted his infidelities—telling Maggie, the protagonist of my novel, to get a life that belonged to her, just her. But often, I supposed if I were honest, my characters were talking about me, a solo traveler in my seventies, shoving my suitcase into an overhead bin and setting off into the unknown, each of them saying, "Who does she think she is?"

I had no idea what words would fill my pages here in France, but I knew I wanted to get rid of disguises and outside voices and dive down into the heart of things — whatever that meant. Writing was like that; you lived with ambivalence and stepped into the unknown.

Before I applied, I'd researched the village of Auvillar. It was on *Le Puy*, one of the many pilgrimage routes that led to the shrine of Saint James in Santiago del Compostela, Spain. The French called all of the pilgrimage routes the *Chemin*, the Way, a Christian path. I thought of Crusaders and wondered whether their armies had passed through Auvillar. My friend, Rabbi Lev, once described pilgrimage as a portal to God, to history, to a source. I thought of a river that began with a trickle, something small that gathered momentum. And power. I thought of shards of pottery, remnants of past civilizations buried deep in the earth. Was pilgrimage a way of bringing truth up through layers of rock and dust and into the light of the present? Or was it the opposite, a way to justify one's beliefs and leave the past and its lessons buried?

I thought of pilgrimage as Christian, then learned Jews have pilgrimages, too. The festivals *sukkot*, *shavous*, and *pesach*, passover, all marked times when Jews traveled to the Temple in Jerusalem to offer sacrifice. After the destruction of the Second Temple in 70 CE, the rabbis transformed physical pilgrimage to celebrations in our homes. You could say that our dining room tables became our altars.

I stood at the opened gate, my mind leaping from pilgrims and pilgrimage to Auvillar's Jewish history during the Second World War. Had Jews lived in the village? Perhaps sheltered here? In *Packing Light*, her collection of new and selected poems, Marilyn Kallet writes of Dr. Hirsch, a Jew who lived in Auvillar during the War. Hirsch being my maiden name, this coincidence of our matching names intrigued me. I corresponded with Kallet and she gave me the name of Dr. Hirsch's son, Jean, a nine-year-old resistance courier then, and now a doctor living in Paris. In my application, I proposed researching and writing a series of essays — hybrid forms that would be part history, part memoir, and part travel — about this boy.

When I had arrived the day before, John, who was married to Cheryl, the resident director, picked me up at the airport in Toulouse. Along our ride, we passed field after field of sunflowers lifting their shaggy orange-yellow heads to the sky. Long dirt drives led to farmhouses, only their roof lines visible from the road. Tall and lanky, with shaggy hair and a gentle demeanor, John spoke softly or not at all. I sat back and watched out my window as we climbed from hilltop village to hilltop village, taking the scenic route, John said. Some villages had public squares, others didn't. John pointed out a public laundry still in existence, but no longer used.

"A public laundry?" I said.

"People used to bring their clothes to outdoor tubs. Auvillar has the remnants of one. You'll pass it as you walk to the village." It was a Sunday and shops were closed. Church bells chimed, and I remembered Sundays in Morristown, New Jersey when I was a child, the closed shops, church bells ringing, then silence. Sunday, *Shabbat*, a day of rest. "So quiet," I said.

My room in the Maison Vielhescazes, MV, the Fellows residence, was on the front of the house and overlooked the street, a narrow park, and the Garonne River. John showed me how to open and fasten my

shutters to the outside of the building. My window opened to the air —
no glass, no screens, life unfiltered.

The room had two twin beds, two low dressers, a chair, and a ward-
robe. A bathroom was down the hall. Two others lived on this floor:
Donna, a composer; and Christina, a novelist. Craig, a sculptor, had a
room downstairs.

The three buildings that comprised Moulin à Nef had names: the
Maison Vielhescazes (MV), named for the man who had once owned it;
La Cloucado, the administration building where Cheryl and John lived
and where Cheryl, an artist, painted; and *Le Cebo,* which housed our
studios. *Le Cebo* translated to onion in Occitan, the old language. How
fitting, I thought. Wasn't that why I'd come here, to peel away layers
and get to the sweet, nearly translucent center?

I closed the gate behind me and listened to the metal lever click
closed. In the park along the Garonne, a woman walked a path and
tossed a stick to her dog, a low-slung creature that looked like a dachshund mix. She would become a familiar and comforting sight. I was a
dog lover, and I missed Lucy and Sam, my two Standard Poodles, both
at home with my husband.

I passed the ninth-century Chapel of Saint Catherine, then a public
water spigot, a fixture commonly found in village squares along the
Chemin. At the edge of the road, two women talked and gestured, one
wearing an old-fashioned apron that looked like a pinafore, the other
wearing a cardigan over a skirt and blouse. Both were short and square
and wore sturdy lace-up shoes like the ones Mama wore. They dyed
their hair burnt auburn, the chosen color of nearly all French women,
no matter their age. Each called to me as I passed. "Bonjour, Madame."
"Bonjour, Madame."

How friendly, I thought, calling back. "Bonjour, Bonjour."

I loved the music of those words uttered over and over, here by a man mixing cement in a barrel, there a woman sweeping her front step. Mama used to sweep the front steps of the yellow stucco house, then the front walk. I felt time like a leaf borne aloft in the wind, curving backward, then forward. Mama was here, the touch of her finger on my wrist. I heard her voice singing what I called her la, la, las, wordless melodies that floated from the kitchen. My pace slowed, and something inside of me rested.

🖋

The road that led to the *centre-ville* narrowed and turned to dirt, and I found myself climbing a steep hill. I zigged and zagged, walking a diagonal path as I did when I climbed steep trails in the White Mountains back home. I passed ancient houses, most of them dating to medieval times. A few sat empty, mortar crumbling, bricks caving as if they could no longer bear the weight of centuries. I also saw signs of repair — scaffolding, a wheelbarrow, a pile of lumber. In the midst of this breaking apart and restoration roses bloomed and a languid stillness hung in the air. In the distance, someone played an accordion, and melody lingered in the air. I could live here, I thought. I could live here.

I came upon the cement tubs John had mentioned, a public laundry in use through the years of the Second World War. I peered down into stagnant water and imagined women coming here to wash their husband's work trousers and their children's overalls, scrubbing on wooden washboards. This was a place to congregate and exchange gossip. A substitute for the beauty parlor. Talk of someone's pregnant daughter. *Little fool.* Or perhaps a hidden Jew. *Did you hear? In the woodshed. He left in the night.*

On a cement wall opposite the laundry, rosemary grew in profusion and cascaded. I picked a sprig, rubbed the plant's needle-like leaves between my thumb and fingers, releasing a minty-piney scent. This wall and this rosemary were my marker, the place where I needed to turn left. The road narrowed and grew even steeper. I came upon Auvillar's round stone market building, a unique structure with open sides, columns, and a red-tiled roof. High in the rafters, pigeons cooed. The day I arrived, I was too late for the market. Next Sunday, I told myself, I will be here.

A colonnade surrounded the main square. Under it, shops, galleries, and doors to houses. The place was mostly empty. A few passersby. A few folks sitting at tables outside a café. Flowers in stone pots bloomed at doorways — geranium, petunias, marigolds, bougainvillea. More flowers bloomed in what were once stone watering troughs. Nasturtium trailed from window boxes. I sat on a low stone wall and breathed the old-world charm and stillness of Auvillar. A scrawny black and white cat, ribs clearly visible, crossed in front of me.

I wandered, walking up and down narrow cobbled streets, some of them mere alleys, one with rounded stones that seemed more ancient than the rest. I learned these were river stones, used before cobblestones. Gardens were everywhere, some out in the open, others hidden in courtyards where I peered through cracks in wooden doors. I stopped in a boulangerie, bought a croissant, and ate as I walked, savoring each flaky, buttery bite. I passed a small market, a *tabac*, a hotel with a flagstone terrace, a pizza parlor, a beauty shop, a few restaurants, a church. I was struck by the absence of any storefront bearing a Jewish name. I'd naively assumed that like small towns in the states, these villages would have housed a few Jewish merchants. I sensed that if Jews lived here now, they remained invisible.

Back at the *centre-ville*, I chose an outside table and ordered a double espresso. Around me, men and women sipped coffee. An older man wearing a cap, the kind men wore here, flat and narrow brimmed, read a newspaper. People smoked and lingered. A few cars were parked next to this patio, but no cars traveled the street. No one held a cell phone to an ear. Auvillar was a *beau village*, a beautiful village, an historic village, and I was here, sipping espresso, thinking without thoughts, dreaming without pictures, floating.

⚬

On Tuesday, Cheryl drove me and the other Fellows to an open market in Valence d'Agen, a village four miles north of Auvillar. I walked past table after table stacked with lettuces — romaine, bib, endive, curly, purple, green. Past tomatoes of various sizes, shapes and colors; past cucumbers and multi-colored peppers. There were freshly dug root vegetables, beets and carrots, turnips and parsnips. I took in color and texture, the smells of dug earth. A vendor lifted a chicken from a hook and as she cleaved the neck, I remembered Mama cleaving the necks of chickens, splitting and quartering, then frying their livers along with pieces of fatty golden skin, turning the pieces into *grivenes*, fatty treats she fed me with her fingers. This must have been the way she grew up, going to open markets, perhaps to sell the vegetables grown on the family farm in that place she called Russ-Poland.

At the market, I bought a whole chicken. The vendor hacked off head and feet. I declined her offer to keep either. I bought leeks, soil embedded in their roots. I bought bright orange carrots and small purple potatoes. Driving back, we passed field after field, all lying fallow. We passed orchards, apple, pear and peach, kiwi. During the War, the Germans took most of this food to feed their soldiers. Even in the countryside, people were hungry. In the kitchen at Moulin à Nef, I unloaded my groceries. I would roast my chicken later.

That evening, all of the Fellows, Craig, Donna, Christine, and I, along with John and Cheryl, crossed the road and walked to Priscilla's for aperitifs in her garden. Priscilla, an American who spent five months of each year in Auvillar, was a landscape architect. The house she rented faced the river and was aptly named the River House. It was early evening just before sunset, that time photographers and

24

filmmakers call the magic hour. I turned for one last glance at golden light bathing the river before following the others inside.

Priscilla's kitchen was a homey space with a wooden table, wooden cupboards, an old refrigerator, and an old stove with a shelf above holding spices. Everyone kiss-kissed the French way.

Priscilla stood at the counter holding a spatula aloft as if it were a conductor's baton. She was a woman who demanded attention; yet, in spite of her stance, something about her seemed familiar. For one thing, we bore an uncanny resemblance to each other, both small-boned with small features and medium-length hair, Priscilla's dyed a rich dark brown, mine mostly gone to gray. We'd dressed similarly, each of us wearing a black skirt and a knit top — Priscilla's was black and white striped with a bateau neck; mine, gray cotton silk. Unlike me, she wasn't married, at least not at this moment, and she had the guts and the means to spend half of each year living in France. Whatever her ties, they did not bind. I found myself attracted to her sure sense of herself.

Lifting a pitcher, Priscilla poured green liquid into a glass demitasse; then, she twisted the lip with a flourish. "Puréed vegetable soup. Very French," she said. She poured six more cups and offered me the tray with all seven cups. "Do you think you can manage?"

I walked toward an opened door. Then, holding the tray with both hands, I stood on a threshold, mesmerized by what I saw: a walled garden where ivy climbed a stone wall and roses bloomed on a trellis. There were dwarf trees and pots with more roses. Although the garden was tiny, there were paths and a cement patio with chairs, and a table covered with a provincial print cloth, each stripe a different floral motif in shades of mustard, forest green, and maroon. On the table, bud vases held roses, and a wicker cornucopia spilled winter squash, apples, pears, nuts, and ripe figs. Plants grew densely, but in a controlled manner. This was the secret garden of my dreams, a hidden world.

A gentle touch at my elbow. "It's what I do, you know, design gardens," Priscilla said.

I stepped down onto a path and made my way to the table where my new friends sat, all engaged in conversation. Donna and Christina leaned away from each other, making room for me and the tray, and just as I was about to set it down, a branch snagged my shirt. I tightened my grip on the tray. Suddenly, Priscilla was at my side plucking me free. "*Prunus cerasifera*, purple leaf plum," she said, pushing the branch aside. "And that one is an *acura japonica*, spotted laurel." She named a *Nerium oleander*, pink oleander, rattling off the Latin and the English in a way that was both off-putting and charming.

John poured wine. I could tell he'd done this before, assuming the manly role of playing host. Our choices were a local red, a local white, or something slightly pink called *le secret de la famille* from Château de Bastide. John took up the bottle and eyed me. "This is the one you should try."

Priscilla shot him a look, but John poured a full glass for me, then half a glass for himself. I felt uncomfortable with my full glass of what was evidently a very special wine. "We tried it last week," Christina said. "You go ahead."

Isabelle and Catherine Orlia, sisters, had made the pink wine at their château. It was cold and crisp, light and dry, but not too dry. "I advise the sisters on their gardens, and they pay me with wine," Priscilla said.

Talk turned to an abandoned orchard where Priscilla picked apples. She picked pears from a different site. She grew grapes on an arbor here in the garden, and harvested fallen black walnuts from different sites around the village. I helped myself to a fresh fig and touched gently, testing for ripeness.

"You like figs?" Priscilla asked.

"Love them," I said.

"Picked this morning," Priscilla said.

"You have a fig tree?"

"Don't need one. They grow everywhere."

Cheryl nodded. "We all pick them."

"Where?" I asked.

"You pass at least six trees on your way up the hill to the village," Priscilla said.

"I do?"

"You know the house with the retaining wall? There's one there. Beyond that there are about three trees on the other side of the road. Before you get to the public laundry."

I hadn't seen a single fig.

"Think Adam and Eve," Priscilla said. She spread her fingers and pointed downward, as if to show me a fig leaf covering Adam and Eve's nakedness.

She placed slices of cheese on rounds of baguette and handed them around. She flattened her palm to her forehead and spoke of a garden she was planning. "*Mon dieu.* She's a Scot, and she wants me to create the perfect English garden. She wants lush. Lush doesn't work here. I'm trying to talk her into native plants. I'm working on a site in Charlottesville."

I interrupted. "Charlottesville, Virginia?"

"Yes, Virginia," she said, dismissively.

Something inside me curled. I knew Charlottesville, and I was looking for connection, a way to strengthen what could be a budding friendship.

Priscilla went on. "I've built walks and drainage canals. I've planted all native plant species. You won't believe the wildlife that came back. And this is in the suburbs. I sat outside and watched a rabbit. I watched birds. And while all of that was going on, a snake lay curled and sunning on a rock. None minded the other."

I liked that. *None minded the other.* An ecosystem, the interconnection of organisms and their environment. Why couldn't humans be like that?

Later, crossing the road and walking back to Moulin à Nef, Christina asked me if I'd met Priscilla before. "No," I said. "Why?"

"You could be sisters," she said.

"You mean because we look alike?" I said.

"Not only that."

She didn't elaborate and I wondered what else she'd noticed, perhaps the way we both moved with deliberate grace. Or, maybe, an undercurrent of rebelliousness with a good-girl quality, the former evident in a sideways glance, a lifted chin, the latter in our measured politeness. Had Christiana picked up on the agitation concealed beneath two smoothed and polished exteriors?

⤜

The next morning in my studio, I stood at my opened window and gazed out at the lazy Garonne. A group of pilgrims passed below, men and women carrying backpacks and striking the pavement with their walking sticks as they tapped their way past the *Rendez-vous des Chasseurs*, Meeting Place of the Hunters, next door. On the *Chemin*, pilgrims walked through forest paths. They walked alongside farmers' fields and they passed through villages and towns on their way to Santiago del Compostela. An old man sitting erect on horseback, his gray hair streaming from under a wide-brimmed hat, came into view. He rode Western, holding the reins in his left hand and clutching the lead rope of a donkey with his right. The donkey carried packs along both flanks. A religious pilgrim? A vacationing pilgrim? Had this man stripped his life down to these two animals and these packs?

I was letting myself get distracted. It was time to find Jean Hirsch.

Inside *le mairie*, the town hall, I was struck by the light. Remodeling had opened this medieval building to the outdoors with particularly

28

wide glass windows and a glass door, all spanning the façade. Sunshine poured in. I asked to speak with Madame Falc. Cheryl told me that her family had something to do with saving Jewish children during the War. She worked here in *le mairie*.

We were two petite women standing on opposite sides of a high counter, trying to make sense of each other. John said she spoke English, so I was going on, telling her I was staying at Moulin à Nef in the Old Port, not realizing that I probably had Moulin à Nef written in fluorescent marker on my forehead. I said I wanted to know about Jean Hirsch, the nine-year-old resistance courier during the Second World War. That was all I had, his name and the names of his father and mother.

Madame Falc glanced back at her desk. She was uneasy. "No, no English," she said.

My French dated from my sophomore year in college, augmented over subsequent years with Duolingo. I bumbled along, saying I understood that during the Second World War a boy had lived in the village with Sigismond, his father the village doctor, and Berthe, his mother. I didn't add that I'd conjured my own story of this family, imagining Doctor Hirsch driving from farm to farm — automobile? horse and buggy? — bandaging wounds, setting bones, delivering babies, and holding the hands of the dying. Or that I'd imagined Berthe, a pretty, dark-haired woman, walking to the boulangerie to buy a baguette, and then walking home.

I also asked about a Jewish cemetery. History lived in those markers. I didn't know the word for cemetery, so I made up a phrase that sounded right, *place de mort*. I pantomimed digging. Madame Falc fixed me in her gaze. I had asked for a place of death, not a place of burial. I bumbled onward. *"Est-ce que les juifs habit à Auvillar maintenant?"*

The word was in the air, *habit*. Wrong verb. *Habit* had something to do with clothing. "Live," I said emphatically, as if coming down hard in English would translate to French. "Do Jews live here now?"

Madame raked her fingers through her short blond hair. "*Non pas maintenant. Les derniers juifs étaient la famille Hirsch.*"

"*Où?* Where? Where did they live?"

"*Là.*"

She pointed, and I looked through the glass at the round market, the colonnade, a row of houses.

"There?" I asked.

"*Oui.*"

"One of those houses?"

"*Oui, oui.*"

"Do you know which one?"

She turned and walked back to her desk. "*Je ne sais pas.*" She had understood me all along.

Was her unwillingness to speak before perfecting a language simply a matter of typical French pride, or was it due to something more?

3

I opened the blue shutters of my studio and fastened them to the outside wall of the building. I stood and pondered the Jean Hirsch story. At home in the States I'd read widely about Jews and Vichy France, Jews and Occupied Paris. After France's stunning defeat and humiliation in May 1940, when the German Army outflanked the Maginot Line — France's line of defense in central Belgium — and marched instead through the Ardennes Forest in southeastern Belgium, surprising the French, and one month later crossed the Seine and entered Paris, General Marshall Pétain signed an armistice with Hitler. Both men divided the country into Occupied and Unoccupied Zones. French pride was crushed, and to this day the French call this defeat *le désastre*.

The French government left Paris and went first to Bordeaux, then to the spa town of Vichy, from where Pétain, World War I hero, sympathizer and newly-transformed Nazi collaborator, governed the Unoccupied Zone until war's end. Ironically, Pétain had earned his heroic stature after defeating the Germans at Verdun during the First World War but later became pro-Nazi.

In reality, all of France was under German control between

1940-1945, no place was safe for Jews — neither Occupied nor Unoccupied zones — although Jews had a better chance of surviving in the south, particularly in a remote village like Auvillar. But in the heart of the village?

I sank down into a makeshift chaise made of simple slatted wood and covered with a thin cushion, sitting inches from the floor. I adjusted a pillow at my back and closed my eyes. I saw colors beneath my eyelids and listened to the buzz of silence. Time past crept into time present like a slow fog. I saw an image that had haunted me since childhood, of men, women and children standing on a forest path, all dressed for travel. In front of them a pit that would become their mass grave. Nazi soldiers holding German Shepherds on short leashes stood beside soldiers with rifles.

I don't remember when I first saw this image. Probably, I was five, maybe six, wandering the living room and drawn to *Life* magazine. I looked inside. I knew those people were Jews, and in spite of what my father said about German Jews being better — "refined," he said — than Polish-Russian Jews, I knew Mama and Papa came from a place they called Russ-Poland, and if they were like those Jews, I was, too.

Over the years, images I'd seen as a child, then later, blended and collaged in memory — photographs, exhibits, books, films, cattle cars, barbed wire, railroad tracks. I remembered a photograph of a boy, maybe three, his hands raised in surrender. Pinned to the lapel of his coat was a six-pointed yellow cloth Jewish Star, the Star of David. I saw myself as that child. This photograph has become an iconic image of loss and inhumanity, which is to say humanity, for it shows what we are capable of doing to one another. I pushed up from the chaise and reminded myself that those mass graves, those railroad tracks, those camps, that child, all belonged to Germany and to Poland. I was nowhere near those lands.

At my computer I searched for Jean Hirsch and found the AJPN website, *Anonymes, Justes et Persecutes durant la periode Nazie dans les communes de France*: Anonymous, Righteous and Persecuted People during the Nazi period in the French communes. In France, villages belong to communes the way towns belong to counties in the States. Auvillar was in the commune of Tarn-et-Garonne. The AJPN, a nonprofit organization headquartered in Bordeaux, collected Second World War testimonies and added them to an open online database. Jean Hirsch's testimony dated from April 27, 2006. He was in his early seventies, then. He began, *"Je m'appelle Jean Hirsch...."* French, it was all in French. I translated what I could. His name. Then, "I had arrived in the region fleeing Paris..."

Arrived in the region? Fleeing Paris.

He and his family were not from this village as I'd imagined. They were from Paris, urban cosmopolitans.

In the early '70s when I lived with my family in Holderness, a rural New Hampshire town, folks said we came from away, and I understood that if you came from away, you didn't belong — would never belong.

The school where I taught was a cement rectangle with a metal roof, noisy when it rained. The building housed grades K-8, all of the school-aged children who lived in town. My classroom looked out on a barren field. One day after school, I sat at my desk and watched snow drift down, tiny flakes dusting the landscape. It was December and my homeroom students had decorated the classroom for Christmas. Paper chains, tinsel, and shining balls adorned a tree. Holderness was a white, Christian town, and at that time we were the only Jewish family that lived there. The two greatest insults kids hurled at one another on the playground were "nigger" and "Jew." I marched the offenders to the principal, and then I announced to each of my classes that I and my family were Jewish. I lectured my classes, saying all of us, black or white, Christian or Jew (there was no talk of Muslims then),

33

were members of the human race, different yet the same, and each of us deserved tolerance and respect. Yet, still conflicted about my own identity, I hung a wreath on my front door and strung lights on a Christmas tree in our living room. That December day as I turned from the window, I was surprised to see Arnold, one of my sixth-grade students, hovering in the doorway. He was a skinny boy with shiny black hair and an unruly lock that skimmed his left eyebrow.

He walked slowly to my desk. "Can I?" he said. He didn't finish his thought. I waited. "Would you?" Another pause.

"What is it, Arnold?"

"I want to see your horns."

On the other side of the bank of windows, snow swirled up from the field, a whirlpool transporting me back to paintings I'd seen of Jews wearing strange hats. I remembered Michelangelo's horned Moses. The notion that Jews had horns fed into the medieval Christian myth of the Jew as a devil, the Jew as evil, and all of that was still alive, still here. This was the mid-'70s, and the boy wasn't joking.

"Arnold, I don't have horns. That is simply preposterous." *Does he understand preposterous?* "Jews do not have horns. Who in the world told you that?"

The next day, he offered a book: *Protocols of the Elders of Zion.* Familiar and unfamiliar. Something distasteful. Something anti-Semitic. I tried to look into his face, but he cast his gaze to the tiled floor. I spoke softly. "Arnold, why are you giving me this?"

"Because of what you said. My father said to tell you to read it."

I thought of his father standing up at a town meeting and expounding on overpaid teachers before voting against the school budget. He suggested firing us all and hiring teachers just out of college at lower salaries. He was deeply religious. Fundamentalist. He ruled his family with an iron fist and punished with a wooden cane. I rarely disciplined Arnold because I knew what waited for him at home.

I told no one about the book, not my principal, not my husband. That night in the den, after my family had gone up to bed, I read a few pages, but I couldn't figure out what I was reading. The wording was dense. Old-fashioned.

The *Protocols of the Elders of Zion* was a fake. The book tells the story of a meeting that was supposed to have taken place. At this non-meeting, Jews plotted to take over the world and destroy Christianity. Who believed this rot? Arnold and his father. Who else?

❧

My computer screen had gone dark. I pressed a key and brought back the AJPN website, and as I eagerly searched for more, the internet yielded. In prewar Paris, Sigismond Hirsch ran a medical clinic. He was political — a man who, with Robert Gazmon, founded the Éclaires Israélites de France, French Jewish Scouts, an ordinary scouting organization before the War, and then a resistance organization during the War. The Scouts printed secret documents, acted as couriers, fought with the Resistance, and moved Jews across borders to Switzerland or Spain. They established a network of safe houses for orphaned Jewish children throughout the south of France, one in the nearby town of Moissac run by Shatta Hirsch Boulé, Sigismond's sister, and Simon, her husband.

Sigismond Hirsch led a resistance group in Auvillar, Berthe working at his side. They turned their nine-year-old son into a courier, a boy riding his bicycle from Auvillar to the safe house in Moissac, delivering false documents concealed inside the hollow tubes of his handlebars. Who would stop a boy riding his bicycle? And what father and mother would put their child in such danger?

Digging deeper into Jean Hirsch's testimony on the AJPN website, I learned that in the fall of 1943, the Gestapo arrested Sigismond and Berthe. Jean Hirsch writes he was not at home on the night of the arrest. He was taking a piano lesson with a priest, and because darkness had fallen, he'd spent the night there. The next morning resistance workers headed him off, saying his father had ordered him to hide out, and so the boy walked to a nearby convent where nuns cared for epileptics and people with Down Syndrome. Jean Hirsch wrote: "Thankfully, they (the Gestapo) were disgusted by the sight of the crazed epileptics who urinated everywhere and the Down Syndrome people who stuck out their tongues. The Germans hurried away, religiously, accompanied by the nuns."

I pondered the words, *religieusement accompagnés par les soeurs*, as if the nuns were fulfilling God's commandment. In a way, they were. I marveled at the courage of these women, for beneath their habits and calm demeanor their hearts must have beat furiously.

And what of the child Jean, hiding and listening?

Good story. But something didn't ring true. How could his father, under arrest, possibly have gotten word to his son? And what of the piano lesson with a priest? Why had it been scheduled so late? Wouldn't the priest, knowing he was teaching a Jewish child, have sent him home well before dark? I was looking for answers, and I found questions. Besides, I didn't trust my French. Our brains love narrative, and so they fill in the blanks, and they embellish. We transpose time. Dreams ooze into reality, and reality oozes into our dreams. How easily we cross borders, conscious to unconscious, time past to time present. Where was the truth of this story?

I emailed Valerie Fert. Back in the States, Rabbi Lev had put us in touch. Through a serendipitous series of events, Lev had flown to Paris to officiate at Valerie's marriage to Thierry. She was French and Jewish; Thierry was French and Catholic, and when Valerie could not find a rabbi in all of France to officiate along with a priest, a friend put her in touch with Lev.

Valerie and I made our acquaintance in the virtual world. She was, she explained, an historian who had specialized in Near East and Bible studies, and she'd earned her master's degree in Jerusalem. She was also interested in France's Second World War Jewish history, and she spoke fluent English. She would be happy to exchange emails. We agreed to meet in Paris at the end of my residency.

I shot her a link to the AJPN website and Jean Hirsch's testimony. I'd translated as best I could, but now I had a native French speaker to help me make sense of the more puzzling parts of this document. Just how widely known were Jean Hirsch and his family? Had Valerie heard of Sigismond and Berthe, the boy's parents? If she had, what did she know of them? Jean Hirsch would be seventy-eight now. Was he living? Could she find out? I wasn't sure why I wanted to know, but something was leading me, and I was following. I closed my computer and decided to explore the countryside. I wanted to walk the roads Jean Hirsch had walked or perhaps ridden on his bicycle.

Earlier, John had drawn me a map and charted out a nearly four-mile loop from the Old Port, up hills, down hills, then into the village and down the steep hill past the rosemary and the public laundry and back into the Old Port. At the crest of the first hill, I stopped to admire an old stone farmhouse. Next to it, a large barn. Across the road, another building with a screened room where a farmer sat drinking what I assumed was coffee. He called out, "Bonjour, Madame."

"Bonjour," I called back. Was he old enough to remember Vichy? Could he and Jean Hirsch have been boys together in this village? Attended the same school? I did not have the courage to ask.

At a plateau, a tree grew close to the road. I looked closely at its leaves and spread my fingers as Priscilla had done. I looked under the leaves. Figs.

I glanced toward the house. All seemed quiet. No cars approached from either direction. I stretched and reached, helping myself to three ripe figs, their skin warm and soft to my touch. At a curve in the road, I glanced back and saw only the roof of the farmhouse. Then, I bit.

My loop led me past the pharmacy with its lighted green cross, up a hill, then left under the clock tower where once this village was gated. As I passed beneath the arch, the tower bell chimed the hour. The bell in the steeple of the Church of Saint Peter echoed. A short street opened out into *la place des halles*. I sat on the low stone wall surrounding the market, my back to the *mairie,* and looked in the direction Madam Falc had pointed. Under the colonnade, houses touched. Which one had belonged to *la famille Hirsch?*

I chose a shuttered house with most of its paint worn away, a house in disrepair with broken windows, where no one lived. I was drawn to a balcony outside a second-story window and a railing where I imagined Jean Hirsch watching for his father's return.

To understand this place better, I joined a village tour. My guide spoke rapid and highly accented English. I didn't catch his name. It began with a D, so for me he was Monsieur D., a short man with white hair and an abbreviated white mustache. We gathered beneath the clock tower and before I had a chance to look up at the bell he had turned and led us down a narrow alley. This was the oldest street in Auvillar and the only one paved with round stones from the river.

We wound our way to a courtyard in front of *l'Église de Saint Pierre.* This was a grand church and I wondered at its size, but churches, particularly in Europe, were not only holy structures, they were statements. In cities and towns I'd visited in France, Spain, and Italy, synagogues either didn't exist or were hard to find. That, too, was a statement. Monsieur D. spoke of Auvillar's long-ago prosperity: two monasteries, Benedictine and Dominican, and an Ursuline convent in the hills. Could these have been the nuns who sheltered Jean Hirsch, the nuns who "religiously" ushered the Gestapo out the door?

38

"Monsieur…" I called. Then, louder. "Monsieur."

He paid no attention. Monsieur D. motioned and the group followed. Had he heard me? Was he avoiding me? Perhaps questioning a tour guide was an American thing, not French. "We will gather there," he said, pointing to an empty square of land. Once a grand château had stood on this site, he said. At the far end, an ancient stone wall guarded a cliff where I'd stood in days past, looking down on the tops of trees and into the countryside. You could see for miles from this place. Had I been the Huguenot Earl who had once lived in that château, I would have seen approaching armies. I also would have lost my battles, for during the religious wars, when Catholics fought Protestants, the château was burned. So was the church. Over the years, it was rebuilt, but not the château. "So, you see," Monsieur D. said.

I did see. The Earl of this vanished château lost his battle to the Church. In Europe, my awareness of religious power itched like a rash under my skin. I thought back to my college years and my English professor, an Anglophile in love with T. S. Eliot. *My house is a decayed house, / and the Jew squats on the windowsill, the owner.* The cliché of the Jew as slum landlord. In class, I bowed my head and sank to my spine. I had similar feelings in art history class when, one day, Professor Taylor put two slides up on a screen side by side, statues flanking the main portal of Notre Dame, Ecclesia and Synagoga. Ecclesia holds her head high and wears a crown. Eyes open, she looks out into the world. Synagoga bows her head. A snake coils and blinds her eyes. Her body curves inward. Recently, I saw those statues, still there, still sending their message.

My senior year, I was one of twelve students taking a class called Life of the Mind, taught by the president of the college. Monday evenings, we trudged up a hill to his house, the largest and loveliest on campus. We sat on couches, chairs, and the rug at his feet as he lectured about the Greeks, the Romans, western Europe, and of course Christianity.

No one mentioned Jews or Jewish history. As a Jew growing up in a Christian world, I understood that history, real history, Christian history did not belong to me. I felt erased. Now, on this tour I had the same feeling.

At the *place des halles*, Monsieur D. spoke of an earlier market on this site, one with an underground silo dating from the Middle Ages. Was that silo still there? Was it possible that Jews had hidden inside during the Second World War? So far, I had heard only Monsieur D.'s prepared spiel. What did he know of Auvillar's Jewish history? I moved to the front of the group. "Monsieur, I understand a Jewish family lived in Auvillar during the Second World War. Very nearby." I pointed. "In one of those houses."

No answer. Determined to be heard, I tried French. "*Une famille juif. La famille Hirsch.*"

For a fraction of a second, his clear blue eyes pierced the air between us. Then he looked past me. I was sure my accent was thick; yet, I was also certain he'd understood. "*Le docteur. Le médecin.*"

"*Ah.*" He moved an index finger in front of his eyes slowly like a metronome. "*Rien de plus.*"

No more.

"Yes. I understand. *Mais quelle maison?* Which house? I want to know which house."

He turned away, tossed words. "*Numéro trois.*"

"*Numéro trois?*"

"*Oui, oui.*"

The vacant house I'd chosen after my walk was *Numéro deux*, number two.

At number three, stone work had been extensive — large building blocks and bricks, all smoothed and newly mortared. A stone archway with detailed carvings framed a polished arched wooden door. The window sash was stained a rich brown. One pair of windows opened out into the plaza like French doors. I left the group and looked inside.

In the living room, a man sat at a corner table reading a newspaper. I saw couches and chairs, a drum set. I had a clear view through an opened back door into a garden. Roses bloomed and climbed an arbor. I imagined Sigismond, Berthe and Jean all sitting at a table and taking afternoon tea. I snapped a photo. Another. I had no shame.

A woman from inside gave me a look and reached out to close the windows. I stared at white lace curtains behind glass and thought about this village during wartime. What had this house looked like then? Clearly, this renovation was recent. How recent? The back garden I'd glimpsed would have been there, maybe the roses, too, hidden from view.

I meandered back to the Old Port, passing the public laundry and the cascading rosemary. I helped myself to another ripe fig and I bit, exposing the fig's burnished pink center and a myriad of tiny seeds. Now I saw them everywhere, these pale green or purple figs hanging under wide leaves that looked like a hand with an open palm.

PART II

4

The forecast was for rain, but for now low-hanging clouds did not mass. In Miradoux, a hilltop village, Priscilla and I posed for pictures, Priscilla wearing jeans, a long-sleeved blue T-shirt, a baseball cap and gloves — because, as she explained, otherwise her hands swelled and her skin became uncomfortably tight. Behind her, the landscape fell away into a patchwork of rolling hills. Crops had mostly gone to harvest, leaving subtle color, shades of tan, rust, and green. Trees grew on hilltops.

I'd bumped into Priscilla the week before on market day in Valence d'Agen. We were blocking the narrow-cobbled sidewalk, and people stepped into the road to walk around us. "Come walk the *Chemin* with me," Priscilla said.

"The *Chemin*," I said, hesitating, although I didn't know why.

"Trust me. You'll want to get out of the Old Port for the weekend. A street fair is taking over. You won't be able to hear yourself think."

Now, in Miradoux, I handed Priscilla my camera, sat on a low stone wall, and looked out from beneath my wide-brimmed hiking hat. Priscilla captured a closed-lip smile, not my usual open-mouthed grin.

I was trying to be sophisticated. To be perfectly honest, I wanted to emulate her, but impish joy shone in my face. Now, I felt that old sensation spilling from the inside out. Whatever doubts I'd harbored — hardly admitting them to myself — about spending two nights and three days with a woman I'd met the week before, vanished like vapor into the air. We shouldered our packs and followed a path alongside a farmer's field, at a leisurely pace. We would walk that day, spend the night in a *gîte*, then walk back to Auvillar on our second day. To our right, patches of tall grass gone to seed. To our left, a row of young trees planted to shield the *Chemin* from a macadam road. There was no traffic. No noise save the buzz of an insect.

A pilgrim, a thin young man with shaggy brown hair and carrying an old-fashioned frame backpack, approached, head bowed perhaps in prayer or contemplation. He passed, wordlessly. The next group dispelled my thoughts of piety. They were a gregarious group of men and women, Germans who spoke French. Priscilla was their focus. Without language, I stood at the edge of a closed circle, watching Priscilla's animated face, her gloved hands gesturing. I thought back to the evening in her garden when we met, Priscilla pouring soup, then lifting the lip of the pitcher with a turn of her wrist, Priscilla brandishing a knife to slice a baguette, every movement theatrical and calculated to draw attention.

I noticed a low-growing tree laden with pale green apples blushed with crimson, each apple maybe three inches in diameter. The last time I saw lady apples I was at a farm stand in Virginia. I remembered a basket of them tucked under a wooden table. When the group of pilgrims moved on, I showed Priscilla the tree. Without hesitation, her fingers darted. She twisted a stem, pulled, then bit. "Did you know lady apples date back to the first century?" she said. "Hardy little fruits, aren't they?"

These apples were so small that Priscilla and I shoved three down into a single pocket. Laughing, we filled a second pocket. As we strolled side by side, I told Priscilla of a gnarled apple tree in my yard at home. "It's been there for years, way before the house was built. It gets fertilized with its own fruit. Plenty of water. But the apples are inedible."

Shrugging, Priscilla pulled another apple from her pocket. "Could have been a miserable apple tree to begin with. You live on the coast, right? All that salt air sitting on leaves makes life hard for a tree." She smiled in a knowing way. "And so, how do you kill a tree? Well, how did the Romans take Carthage?"

I had no idea how the Romans took Carthage, had no idea they'd even taken Carthage, but I liked the thought that Priscilla did.

"By putting salt in the soil," she said.

My tree, planted years ago, had endured not only harsh temperatures, but indeed, air-borne salt as well. Yet every spring the tree budded, then blossomed, and every fall it bore its miserable, wormy and misshapen fruit. It might not have fed me, but it fed worms, birds, chipmunks, and squirrels. I loved that tree. "Do you think it's dying?" I asked.

"Slowly," Priscilla said.

The Commune de Flamarens began, as all these villages seemed to begin, with a steep climb to a height of land. We approached through a narrow street with ancient stone buildings rising like walls. At the ruin of a church, a wooden sign announced a restoration site, but I saw little evidence of recent work. We entered the ruin. Dust choked the air. This place felt and smelled long abandoned. The roof was mostly gone, and remnants of gothic arches and vaulted ceilings reached to the sky. I felt strange inside this wreckage that was neither sanctioned ruin nor rebuilt cathedral.

Along one wall, a wooden stage. Who performed here? Everything about this ruin was out of kilter — piled planks, stacked boxes, a wooden bar with barstools. Off to one side, a small table with chairs. Priscilla and

I contemplated lunch, but neither of us wanted to eat inside this gutted wreck.

Leaving the church, or what was left of it, we spied a grassy knoll with tables and chairs. On the other side of the road, a massive stone château with a turret hindered our view. We moved our chairs to see around it. Shadowed hills rolled under clouds. Priscilla pulled a baguette from her pack. She rummaged and extracted two cans of tuna in tomato sauce, one for each of us. I'd brought a wedge of cheese. We were alone, not a pilgrim or villager in sight. Quiet filled the air. "Tell me about those pilgrims," I said.

"The Germans? They come every year."

"Religious?"

"*Comme si, comme ça.* They thought we were very strong, that we'd walked all the way to Santiago and now were walking back."

Until that moment, I hadn't known we were walking in the wrong direction, away from the shrine of Saint Jacques, not toward it. How fitting for a Jew.

A drop of rain fell. And another. We pulled jackets from our packs and thrust our arms through the sleeves. The rain stopped. Frustrated, I said to Priscilla, "Oh, let's keep them on."

"*D'accord.*"

Leaving the Commune de Flamarens, we descended a hill and passed houses with low stone walls where roses bloomed. I caught the scent of jasmine and thought of gardens at home in Maine, lush and well-tended.

"Gardens are organic, you know," Priscilla said. "Soil moves. Plantings change. Take architecture. You finish a project and afterward, it's all downhill. The paint chips; the rug gets stained; somebody tracks mud on the floors. When you design a garden, you design for the future. Time works on a garden and it transforms."

Time as transformation, not an end. I liked that.

Suddenly, Priscilla's voice grew urgent. "Sandell, where's your camera? Can you get it?" I took off my backpack and dug until I found my camera. "There. That one," Priscilla said, pointing to a distant hill where three trees formed silhouettes against the sky. "The one that looks like a Mohawk."

I saw it, a tree sculpted by wind and rain, its crown the shape of the haircut. I took a few pictures.

"I think she'll like it. And it will work," Priscilla said.

"What will work? Who will like it?"

"My client. Trees planted just like that."

The Scot, the woman who'd hired her to design and plant an English garden here in France, the one who wanted lush. A catch in my belly. Priscilla was using me, first by sending me to the pharmacy for items she needed, then putting me up to asking John for a ride, and now by having me take photographs for her design. She was researching. I was researching too. So why did I feel this way?

"You'll send them to me when we get back, right?" she said.

She knew I would.

After spending the night in our *gîte*, we set out at about eight the next morning, stole a few figs from a nearby tree, and entered a darkened vestibule inside the *Chappelle de Saint Antoine*, an impressive church, again built on a height of land. Priscilla translated from a wooden plaque. "The pilgrim meets himself, and he meets others, and he meets his god in the respect of being of things, of nature, and which is offered to him each day. Light and then lighter, he allows himself to grow and he lacks nothing."

"In the respect of being of things." What did that mean? Ah, because the pilgrim becomes part of what he sees, "he meets his god" in nature and in what is offered each day. Interesting — "his god." Not God. As

49

for God, I was mostly a non-believer. I say mostly because sometimes I prayed, thanking God for a spectacular day or a lost mitten miraculously found. I felt thankful. I felt mystery. Was this God?

Leaning, Priscilla palmed open a heavy wooden door. We stepped into gloomy silence. As my eyes adjusted to the dark, I noticed frescoes. This was an old painting dating from the fourteenth century recently exposed, a sign said. Although the pigment was faded and the painting incomplete, I made out a group of wealthy gentlemen in the lower left. I saw peasants dressed in short tunics and wearing sandals. All were pilgrims. I wondered if in the restoration, restorers had taken off layers of paint, leaving what looked like an artist's sketch. Electric lights on timers, some high in a golden chandelier, turned on, then off, moving the fresco into shadows.

I was surrounded by iconic art, paintings in golden frames, alcoves with statues of Mary, statues of Jesus, of Mary and Jesus, of angels, saints, and Jesus again. Too much Jesus always got to me, and I was seeing a lot of Jesus. A few other pilgrims entered, all of us walking carefully and noiselessly.

A glass case held a relic, a silver casting shaped like an arm with what appeared to be precious stones. Priscilla stood in front of the case, looking intently. At the silver? At the stones? I whispered, "I'm Jewish. I don't get relics. Is that supposed to be Saint Anthony's arm?"

"I think there's a bit of bone," Priscilla said.

"You're not serious."

"You say that a lot."

As I stared at that silver arm encrusted with fake jewels the size of dimes — they must have been fake — deeply held grievances surged. I knew about Saint Anthony. He spent twenty years in the desert. He saw visions. The devil came to him as a black boy with flashing eyes and fiery breath. This black devil was half-man, half-ass, and he had horns. The church transferred those characteristics to Jews. I thought

50

of Arnold, that fifth-grader asking to see my horns. I saw a reflection of my broad-brimmed hiking hat in the glass, Christian history colliding with Jewish history. "I can't believe this stuff still exists," I said. "That people worship pieces of bone. This is cultish. Primitive. Divisive."

Quick to understand, Priscilla clarified, "Because it implies that my cult has the highway to God and yours doesn't? Is that what you're saying?"

"Exactly."

Had I thought my own pluralistic views of religion would protect me from the *Chemin's* history, Crusaders marching to the Holy Land and killing infidels along the way, both Muslims and Jews? All day yesterday and today, as I walked with Priscilla, people assumed I was Christian. Raised to disappear inside that larger culture, I let them. What was I supposed to do, cry out, Hey, look at me, I'm not who you think I am?

As I turned away from the glass case, I wondered if I, a Jew, should be walking this Christian path. Or was I truly a pilgrim now, stripped bare and seeing a reflection I didn't like?

Priscilla touched my elbow. "I don't let it bother me, Sandell."

What? What didn't she let bother her?

Leaving the church, Priscilla and I walked in silence, single file. We walked and walked. Now, sitting on a knoll, the village of Auvillar appeared below, red-tiled roof tops, the clock tower with its bell that sounded the hour, the steeple of *l'Eglise de Saint Pierre*, each like a photo on a postcard. I leaned back onto my elbows and closed my eyes seeking ease, but I couldn't put Saint Anthony, his arm, and the Crusaders to rest. Beside me, Priscilla sketched. I listened to the sound of her pencil meeting paper, staying on paper, coloring in. That scratching pencil felt like an itch in the center of my back. The pencil stopped. "Ready?" Priscilla said.

I blinked my eyes open. I thought of my naiveté that day in the *mairie* when I asked, not only about Jean Hirsch, but about a Jewish cemetery. The only cemetery was beside the church. Jews would not have been buried there, not inside the gates, not inside a Christian cemetery. This tradition went back centuries, and mostly it still held. I knew that. Why hadn't I paid attention? I pushed myself to my feet.

"Feeling better?" Priscilla asked.

"Much," I lied.

In my bedroom, I leaned out the window to close my shutters. All remnants of the street fair were gone. No vendors, no tables displaying their wares. The Old Port had descended into its usual sleepy stillness, and I felt as if I were swimming through the complicated current of a dream. A street lamp lighted the road. This, too, was the *Chemin*, the Way, passing under my window and leading up the hill and into the *place des halles*. In the morning, pilgrims would tap their way past and I would hear the sounds of their walking sticks. Whatever their path, it was not mine; yet, together our footsteps dropped down into centuries.

5

The moon was bright and moving toward fullness. Puffy white clouds hung low, and above the clouds was the deep French blue of the sky. We sat at a table on a patio outside Moulin à Nef. Christine had prepared a chicken curry, rice, and a salad. This was the way we arranged our dinners, each of us taking a turn to cook for the others. That way we had more time in our studios. Cheryl cooked on Wednesdays, a festive meal to which she invited local guests. On weekends we foraged. Always, food was in abundance. On the table: a plate with cheese, goat, sheep and cow, soft and hard, a fresh baguette, a bowl with local grapes, another with nuts from nearby trees. And, of course, the obligatory bottles of local red.

The chairs and table were made of that ubiquitous plastic, the table covered with a plastic cloth; yet, in France even plastic had its charm. John poured wine. A man sitting across from me reached and offered his hand. "I am Robert," he said, pronouncing his name the French way, "Ro" as in "row your boat" and "bear" like the animal.

I took his hand. "*Enchantée.*"

Robert had worked in a nearby nuclear power plant before retiring in this village. These days, he worked with metal. Athough nearly bald with gray at his temples, he was handsome, with a straight nose, inquisitive gray eyes, an impish smile. Robert wore black-framed glasses. My father, too, had been a handsome bald man who wore glasses. That day, as I walked from my studio to the kitchen to brew coffee, I had watched from a distance as Robert and Craig assembled Craig's blue metal sculpture on a hill behind Moulin à Nef. The mesh sculpture was triangular in shape — think the Pope's miter or a heart. There would be space inside for a circular bench, a place to sit and contemplate or perhaps dream. All day long the two men had measured, calculated, and soldered. Craig had needed Robert's soldering expertise.

At this table of English speakers, Robert, too, spoke our language and talk turned to his talent for working with metal. In a workshop on his farm, Robert fashioned precision titanium knives. He pulled one out of a pocket and set it on the table. I never thought I'd say a knife was beautiful, but this one was — sleek and shining, its case engraved with what looked like hieroglyphics. He opened the blades, honed to what seemed perfection. All of us looked. None touched. He told a story of making cigar cutters for a special order. "I notified my customer," Robert said. "I say to him the cutters are ready, and he says to me, 'But I have stopped smoking.'" What did he do? He traveled to Paris and visited cigar shops, where he sold his inventory. "Suddenly, I was in the cigar cutter business," Robert said.

"But no longer?" Donna asked.

"No more." He closed the blades of the knife and, as he was about to slip it back into his pocket, I opened my hand. "May I see?"

He centered the knife on my palm, and I felt its delicate balance and its heft. I looked at the strange markings like symbols of a lost and mysterious language. I met his gaze and something sparked between us. If I were inclined to take lovers… I let my thought fall off. I was just flirting, nothing more.

"So, you are a writer?" he said. Craig must have given Robert a run-down on each of us: the composer, the novelist, and the writer. "You are writing a book?"

"Not a book. Essays," I said.

"Like Montaigne?"

"I wish."

The next day, when Priscilla appeared in the kitchen of the MV to hang a flyer on the refrigerator for another soirée in her garden, I told her I'd met Robert. Did she know him? He seemed interesting. She leaned against the refrigerator. "You should interview him," she said. "His father was a gendarme who retrained German police dogs after the war."

"Priscilla, that doesn't make sense. Why would the French retrain German dogs? Besides, how long does a dog live?"

What did I want with a false lead? I was interested in Jean Hirsch.

She shrugged. "It's what he told me."

"How well do you know him?"

She gave me a sideways look. "Let's say we were friends. Very good friends. It was lovely while it lasted."

I pondered her stories. The one untold, in which she and Robert had been lovers; the one told, about the dogs. Would the Germans have left their dogs behind? Would the dogs have needed to learn French commands? Pretty doubtful. True or not, Robert's father had lived through the war. Would Robert have insights on Vichy, either here or nearby? Had he heard of Jean Hirsch?

I met Robert in front of the *mairie*, where a pottery fair had taken over the market plaza. It was overcast. Robert wore gray trousers, a short stylish raincoat, a golf cap with a narrow brim, and a scarf tied nattily at his neck. As we walked from booth to booth, I asked him about his father and those German police dogs. "Who told you this?" he asked.

"Priscilla," I said.

"Ah, Priscilla," her name a sigh of doubt and resignation. Perhaps, his folly. "Yes, my father trained one dog. This dog did not like me. My sister, she can lie down with this dog in his cage. To me he goes like this." Robert bared his teeth. "This dog had nothing to do with the retreating German Army. My father trained this dog after the war. That was when he became a gendarme. This is important to me, that he became a gendarme afterward."

Important to me, too. His father was not involved in round-ups and deportations. "And during the War?" I asked.

"He was a soldier on the Maginot Line. Captured by the Germans. They took him to Germany. He escaped. This made him a hero."

"That he escaped?"

"This was not easy, you know."

Chastised with good reason, I nodded.

Together, Robert and I studied a large ceramic bowl, narrow at the bottom, wide at the rim — a difficult construction. The potter, a woman with curly brown hair fading to gray, quickly discerned that I spoke English. Years before, she'd worked in Cambridge, England as an au pair. She was happy to speak English again, and so she talked about the nature of clay and about the coils she hand rolled, shaping and smoothing, first with a wooden tool and then with her fingers. She touched the bowl's wobbly rim. "I do not turn on a wheel. I prefer to build by hand. I am closer to the spirit of the clay this way."

My son Andrew was a potter, and he too preferred hand-building to a wheel. I breathed in color and shape, charcoal shading to gray, wobbly curves. Clay was earth and earth was bone. Memory. Footprint.

Thumb inside the smoke-colored bowl, index finger curling outside, Robert ran his touch around the rim. I'd watched Andrew test clay the same way, looking for both flaws and consistency. I remembered weighing Robert's knife in my palm. I'd felt an instant connection, not only to the man but his artistry. Like him, I wanted to touch the potter's bowl, to feel sensation moving from fingertips to hand to arm and through my body, but the vessel was large and I was afraid. Clay was fragile. I didn't want to touch an invisible fissure. I settled for sight — the smoky gray clay, the faint marks of the potter's tools, the beauty of imperfection.

Robert stepped up to a table with vases and mugs, all shaped like toucans and shining with highly glossed glazes, red, green, yellow, black and orange. Garish, I thought, ready to walk past, but because Robert was looking, I looked, too. The pieces were whimsical. Delightful. I gravitated to a booth with contemporary shapes, square mugs and square plates as brightly glazed as the toucans. I looked at jewelry. Robert looked, too. We poked our heads inside a tent where children sat at wooden tables shaping clay. If Dick were traveling with me, he would have tired of these booths and mumbled something about finding a bench, where later I'd find him under a tree, reading one of his John Grisham novels.

Robert spoke of our five senses: sight, smell, hearing, taste and touch. "We can lose them all except one. Touch." I wasn't sure about that, but I didn't want to interrupt. "Always I touch. I think I do this because I cannot smell."

"You can't smell?"

He turned to face me. "I am telling you this. I do not know why I am telling you this."

I thought of things Robert had not smelled — a pot of his mother's simmering stew, his ex-wife's perfume, his girlfriend's musky scent.

"This is my secret. I am telling you."

Secrets tie and bind. I didn't know why he was telling me, either.

Later, inside Robert's stone farmhouse, I sat nearly engulfed by an oversized worn brown leather armchair. Robert called this room "a man's place." Magazines staggered in piles on the floor; books leaned in uneven stacks on shelves, the shelves themselves heaving toward their centers. Robert sat on the couch, elbows resting on his knees. I was curious about his childhood. He was born after the war; yet, I wondered what he'd absorbed. Seven years older than Robert, I remembered kids in my neighborhood turning sticks into guns and shouting, "You're dead! I got you!" Always, the dead were Nazis. Always, the victors were the Americans. I studied Robert's hands in repose, his long fingers, the whorls of his knuckles. "Robert, when you were a child, did you play war?"

"Of course. Of course, I played like this."

He rode memory's current, telling me of a visit to his grandmother's house and climbing a flight of stairs to her... He paused. *"Grenier. Grenier."*

"Grenier?"

"Yes, yes. How do you say?"

We pantomimed. "Ah, attic."

"Attic," Robert repeated. "I found this hand gun. I brought it down. It was my father's." A pensive look crossed Robert's face. "I don't know why, but all of my life I have been attracted to guns. Big-caliber guns." He drew his hands apart.

His attraction to guns surprised me. I scooted to the edge of my seat. "But you are peaceful."

"Yes, I am peaceful, but I like guns. Yesterday I was at my shooting club. I have my sporting license. Shooting is good for me. It makes me patient."

I thought about taking aim, measuring distance with your eye, and calculating trajectory, not once, but over and over. "But I am not able to shoot an animal," Robert said. "When I was a boy, I went fishing with my father maybe three or four times. I caught maybe three or four fish in my life." He pursed his lips in that French way. "All by accident."

Robert told me his father used to fish the Loire, the river that flowed through Nevers, the medieval town where his family lived until he was eight. During the war, the Germans occupied Nevers, and the Allies bombed it heavily. For years these Allied bombings of French cities and French civilians were an untold story. The French knew of course, but not us. I doubt many Americans know the extent of those bombings, even today. Robert's parents had lived through sirens, bombs, explosions, cries for help. They'd foraged for food; everyone had. What of the Jews? What did his parents know of the Jews? What did they see?

"*Personne ne parle pas*," Robert said. No one says. "Afterward, they protected us by their silence. I have no memory of the *Shoah*. Later, I learned."

After the war, truth went underground, buried by what became known as the French silence, De Gaulle claiming that all of France had been resistant, a myth that traveled across the sea to the States. At home, we put forth our own wartime myth, our government telling us we'd done all we could to help the Jews. We hadn't.

No memory and no one making memory. Robert and his ex-wife had brought their children up inside both the larger silence and the personal silence. Telling your children about collaboration, defeat, and your family's humiliation was not a narrative you wanted to pass on. Yet, in graduate school, when Robert's son Nicolas wrote his master's thesis, he chose as his subject the liberation of the camps. "He visited Auschwitz," Robert said. "For years I did not know this about my son. Why I did not know this?"

Truth like water seeps through invisible cracks.

⤺

Another day, Robert and I sat on the terrace of the *Hotel de l'Horloge*. He wore a striped blue wool sweater with a collar and three buttons open at the neck, well-used jeans and soft suede moccasins. He turned an espresso spoon from end to end. "Now you see what I am saying about Communism and Fascism both using the same way to kill people."

We were discussing *Bloodlands,* by historian Timothy Snyder, and Robert was speaking of the way Snyder linked Hitler and Stalin, arguing that each of their ideologies used many of the same weapons, particularly starvation, as ethnic cleansing. What struck me about Snyder's work was that even though he gave these atrocities a broad framework, he didn't diminish Hitler's war against the Jews. For me, this was essential. The *Shoah* was not one in a long line of genocides. It was unique. The killing of Jews had no political or economic justification. It was not a means to an end. It was an end in itself. Never before and not since has the world seen such systematic, bureaucratic evil, an efficient murder machine with the intent of exterminating an entire people, not just from one particular place but from the earth.

At Auschwitz, Jewish musicians played as the trains arrived and disgorged men, women and children. Blinded by the first light they'd seen in days, maybe weeks, these disoriented, filthy, frightened and starving people heard music. They saw gardens and white trucks with large red crosses. This was pure theater, designed to move the Jews obediently toward *selection* — labor or death. I wanted Robert to understand this. "Robert," I said, "the *Shoah* and Stalin's starvations weren't the same."

He tented his fingers. "This question *juif,* the *Shoah.* This story is often in mind in media, the large media, TV, literature, books. In France, the non-Jewish populace observes, hears…" He paused. "We think the Jewish community has a kind of hand on the media to make reference to the Nazi period and to remind the non-Jewish populace they were victims."

Jews playing the victim card.

He rested a hand on my arm as if to say, nothing personal, no offense. But I did take this personally. I was part of this Jewish community, the living and the dead.

"Some pretend the *Shoah* did not exist. We have the proof. We cannot say it did not exist. Le Pen says the *Shoah* is a detail of the story," Robert said.

In 1987, the ultra-conservative French politician Jean-Marie Le Pen caused an outrage with those remarks. He did not deny the *Shoah*, but he did deny its importance in history, diminishing it to a mere detail. He never rescinded his remarks.

"You don't believe him?" I said.

"Of course, I do not believe. What I keep in my memory, what historians do not say, is *the Shoah* was the result of the Nazi ideology about Jews."

But that was what historians *did* say. The Nazis tapped into a European anti-Semitism that stretched back to the First Crusade, the single event that marked the beginning of systematic genocides and mass expulsions based on religion. The difference with the Nazis was that they turned a religious bias into a race bias, and race meant blood. Never mind that race, too, is mythology.

"Fifty million people starved to death," Robert said. "Even my son does not know about Mao Zedong. Why my son does not know?" His son, a filmmaker, a musician, a man he called "the intellectual." Robert gestured broadly. "Our media was able to *cache*..." He paused. "How do you say?"

"Hide."

"Hide," he said. "This kind of *travail*..."

Travail, work, but also difficulty or anguish.

"... all so our governments could open relations with China."

Relations with China — wasn't that Nixon in the seventies? "Robert..." I said, but I couldn't break in. He was on a roll, talking about Vietnam, Pol Pot, Cambodia, and the American Indian genocide, which he said Americans didn't think of as genocide. "But this was a genocide. Do you see?"

61

I did see — starvation, disease, and forced marches to arid lands, all of our weapons the same, Andrew Jackson, Martin Van Buren, Stalin and Hitler. I also saw a side of Robert I hadn't seen before, his vehemence as he spoke of Syria and Assad. He leaned close and narrowed the physical space between us. "Assad will look like a hero compared to the atrocities committed by the other side." That week, in *Paris Match*, horrible photos of rebel brutality. "And the editors, they say they are printing the less horrible." He took up his coffee cup and held it mid-air. "Barbarity is in our genes, eh?"

I almost believed him. I didn't want to believe him.

Robert spoke of a hunt in South Africa. Early in his career, he'd lived and worked there. On the hunt, a herd of gazelle, a word the same in English and French. Beautiful, graceful animals with doe eyes and swept-back ... Robert made a swooping gesture with his hand.

"Horns," I filled in.

"*Voil*à," he said.

He talked of the kill, of being present for the skinning, the butchering, the celebratory eating and drinking.

I thought of *Le Rendez-vous des Chasseurs*, Meeting Place of the Hunters, next door to Moulin à Nef. Saturday and Sunday mornings, men parked their pickups at the curb. In the beds of their trucks, hounds howled inside their cages. I remembered a dead boar on the sidewalk, and later, as I walked past a partially opened door, I saw those same men sitting at a long table feasting, laughing, joking, and pouring wine.

I spiraled down into Robert's litany of barbarity, a hell of mass murder — Nazi Germany, Stalin's Russia, Mao's China, Assad and Syria and so many more — barbarity on a nearly unimaginable scale. In our talk, we lost the *Shoah*. I didn't want to lose the *Shoah*. Each of those murders was a life — a woman, a man, a mother, a father, a lover, a doctor, an actor, a child, a budding musician, a sister, a brother. I was a Jew, a daughter, a wife, a mother, a grandmother, and I felt close to each of those lost lives. Snyder retrieves their voices as they speak from diaries and scraps of paper tossed from cattle cars or found in cracks between bricks in prison cells. He writes, "It is for us as humanists to turn the numbers back into people. If we cannot do that then Hitler and Stalin have shaped not only our world, but our humanity."

I wanted Robert, my friend, to think this way, too. I wanted him to *see* French gendarmes arresting Jews and loading them into cattle cars. I didn't want a whirring blender of mass murder. I wanted footprints. A mark on the earth.

"I am *libéral*," Robert said.

He pronounced the word the French way. *Libéral* was not liberal. In France if you were *libéral*, you were Palestinian friendly, and if you were Palestinian friendly, you couldn't be Israeli friendly, too. According to Valerie, this was a natural way of life here. In France if you were not for somebody, you were against him. Or her. It was impossible for the French to have an argument and feel the frustration of each side. Apparently, this was the reason the French had such a bad agreement after the First World War. "The French wanted to crush Germany. They were motivated by revenge. The French don't negotiate, they strike," Valerie said. If all people felt that way, how were we, either individually or collectively, to build bridges of reconciliation?

Robert said, "The media is for, not against Israel. They often interview Jewish journalists. We feel our media is not under control, but..."

Robert conflated Israelis and Jews, and this anti-Zionism was the new anti-Semitism. The two concepts were not identical, and often the former was used as a pretext for the latter. Criticizing Israel is not anti-Semitic, but condemning Israel for certain practices and failing to condemn others for those same practices is anti-Semitic. My gut tightened. I didn't know if there was room in our friendship for these differences in understanding.

"I used to be for Israel," Robert said. "The small country fighting the bigger countries."

"But now…"

Now the French, much of Europe, and certain groups in the States cast Israel in the role of oppressor. In a reversal, Israel is pictured in cartoons as a Goliath figure, the Palestinians as David, and this, too, reinforced old stereotypes of Jews as controllers of money and media, bringing to mind Vichy France's anti-Semitic propaganda. Back home I'd read about an exhibition that opened in Paris on September 5, 1941. Titled "The Jews and France," the show depicted Jews as a criminal race responsible for all of France's ills. Stereotypical images purported to tell Parisians how to recognize a Jew. An estimated 200,000 people visited the exhibit and breathed in Nazi propaganda. Without biases of their own, could this propaganda have taken hold? I thought of France's large immigrant populations, particularly Muslims, and of France's deep-seated xenophobia. I took a shaky breath. "Robert, do you have Jewish friends? Are there Jews in your life?"

He hesitated. "I have a memory of meeting one girl a long time ago. She was a teenager. I was twenty-two."

I didn't press for details of this memory. I wanted to imagine an innocent flirtation — a teen-age girl and an older boy who was not quite a man.

Robert lifted a metal key ring from the table and slid keys, first one, then another and another. "In relations, honestly, I don't come across Jewish people. Maybe I meet somebody, but I don't know he is Jewish. I am with people who speak about Jews more than people who are Jewish. This is an important point to observe — to hear people speaking about the Jewish community always to criticize. Few people say, 'Look at this doctor, this engineer, he is Jewish, he is so good.' Often they speak in a bad way."

I thought about Robert listening to his friends and keeping silent.

Until this moment, he hadn't understood what he was hearing was anti-Semitic talk. I wasn't sure he'd use the word anti-Semitic, but I sensed he'd gained insight.

Robert stopped sliding keys. "Why the United States is so much for Israel?"

"Not everyone is. There's a lot about Israel I don't like — the settlements, the ultra-Orthodox, the wall, the divisions of Palestinian lands and Israeli lands, the present conservative government, what amounts to apartheid. I think there should be a two-state solution, but I don't think that's possible anymore. I don't know if it ever was possible."

Robert lifted the cuff of his sweater and looked at his watch. "I talk too much. Always, I talk too much."

He stood. Was this the end of our conversation? In spite of my earlier doubts, I wanted this friendship. I wanted Robert's thoughts on France's complex Jewish history. I wanted to know more about the French, their attitudes, their biases. He and I needed to overcome these obstacles. Standing beside him, I touched his arm. "It's complicated about the United States and Israel. I don't understand, either."

He didn't speak. I gathered my notepad, my pen, my iPhone, and my purse. I didn't want to leave like this – without resolution. I searched for something to say, then blurted. "Robert, will you show me your workshop?"

"You want to see where I work?"

"I really do."

❧

A few days later, when I climbed up into Robert's pickup, a thirteen-year old Citroen Berlingo, a Beethoven sonata blasted from hidden speakers. We drove south, out of town, then turned right. This was my morning route. The figs I'd stolen when I'd arrived in the village had been his. He laughed when I told him.

Climbing from the truck, he hurried around the front and opened my door. "*Voilà*," he said. "Still, I do not understand why you want to see the place where I work."

I stepped down. To see where a person worked was to see the person. "Just curious," I said.

We paused at Robert's pond, a large black plastic oval tub, the plastic mostly concealed by a low stone wall Robert had built. Lilies floated and goldfish swam out from under the wide green pads. Robert had emailed a photo of a neuphar in bloom, an Egyptian lotus, an ephemeral flower that lasted only three days. A divinely fragrant flower Robert could not smell. Now, it was gone.

In his vegetable garden, tomatoes lay on the ground, vines tangling. "I thought I would have tomatoes, but then the weather turned wet. So much rain," Robert said. Squash, too, had shriveled and died, along with cucumber and eggplant. Not borage, a hardy plant with dusky prickly leaves and clusters of clear blue star-shaped flowers.

Robert's workshop was a free-standing building about twenty feet from his house, a single room. My nostrils flared at the smells of metal and dust. I saw disorder and chaos, spools of wire, metal cylinders, sandpaper, wooden boxes, screwdrivers, and hammers of all sizes covering nearly every surface. Metal shavings formed heaps under large machines, one with a drill hanging like a giant's snaggletooth. So many cranks, wheels and levers. Passages were narrow. Robert named a lathe, a milling machine, and a *panthographe*, a word neither of us could translate. Cabinets with slim drawers lined the aisles. Chains and wrenches hung from ceiling hooks. I didn't want to snag my loosely knit sweater, so I held my arms close to my body and stepped sideways. I tasted grime.

Robert touched a metal cylinder, releasing a mushroomy, metallic odor he could not detect. "It is a mess here, I know. Lately I have not been working."

When a metalsmith did not grind, when a potter did not shape clay, when a writer did not find words, something was not right.

Robert slipped his hands into his pockets and walked deeper into his workshop. "Sometimes, I feel a little bit in jail with my knives. I'm not able to do anything else. It's life. I know it."

That closed-in feeling of depression. I knew it, too. Sometimes, something inside of me closed down. My arms and legs grew heavy. I slogged through my day feeling as if I were pushing aside heavy curtains. I waited for the oppressive weight to lift.

Robert picked up a flat unfinished knife, handle and blade on the same plane. Eventually the knife would have dimension and weight, a case with etchings like the hieroglyphics on the knife I'd held in my hand. And a number. Robert counted his knives, and he knew who owned each one. He held the nascent knife with fingers and thumb, displaying it for my photo. Setting it down, he spoke slowly, "Maybe, soon, I will work again."

All of my life I'd been drawn to men like Robert who hinted of melancholy and what I called a touch of the poet — my high school sweetheart, then a college romance. Instead, I married a practical man, a businessman, a decent man, a funny man with a quick wit that could dig like a needle looking for an embedded splinter. Always, he had my back. But he was not a man to bare or share his feelings. We did not read the same books. He said, plainly, "You'll have to find that somewhere else."

So, I did.

6

At a corner house on *la place des halles*, a few doors down from *le mairie*, I peered into another window, but I couldn't see through a lace curtain into the interior. The house had two front doors. I knocked on one, then the other. I turned the key of an old-fashioned bell; no one answered. I knocked on the glass. The door to my left opened. A voice said, "Ah, I did not hear."

Gerhard Schneider was a large man with a wide, friendly face. He wore a loose-fitting woolen jacket over a striped cotton button-down shirt, tan trousers, and tan slippers. Both Cheryl and John said that if I wanted to know about Jean Hirsch, I needed to meet Gerhard. He and his wife Mary Jo were academics — Gerhard, a Catholic theologian and a philosopher; Mary Jo, also a Catholic, was a teacher of French literature. Early in their marriage they set out to bridge their two cultures. In retirement they founded the *Société Auvillaraise Culturelle Franco-Allemande*, bringing art, music and literature to Auvillar and surrounding villages. Another interest of Gerhard's was Auvillar's Jewish history.

"You have been waiting long?" Gerhard said.

I smiled at his reversed syntax, so like Mama's Yiddish that my apprehension about knocking on a stranger's door melted away. German was his first language, French his second, English his third. He escorted me down a long hallway, fingers at my back and lightly guiding me in that way of men of my generation.

At the end of a narrow corridor I stepped down into a room that stretched horizontally. This was an old house, dating from the fifteenth century, and I marveled at the ancient stone and brick. At one time, this space was divided; then, Gerhard and Mary Jo bought the house next door and broke down walls. Support arches marked off a kitchen, parlor, and this dining room where we sat. The house was also a *gîte*; Gerhard and Mary Jo offered lodging to pilgrims.

Recent days had turned from summer hot to cloudy and cold, and I was grateful for a fire burning in a cooking hearth at my back. I smelled time in the acrid scent. I felt the ghost of a woman entering this room, then standing at the hearth stirring a pot of stew, perhaps at the moment Columbus set sail to search for the spices of India. Time here is like a string that pulls through centuries.

On the table a cloth with varied patterns: stripes, paisleys, solids and flower prints, their common theme colors of rose, burgundy, pink and white, colors repeating in panels hanging listlessly from a rod at a window and on cushions. There were too many chairs, too many sideboards and low chests of drawers, too many knickknacks and decorative ceramic plates, pitchers and bowls. Nothing was of a piece; yet, everything belonged. Although Gerhard and I had exchanged emails, we hadn't met until this moment. Still, I felt kinship and comfort in his presence.

Without asking, Gerhard set a mug of coffee at my place. I looked down into my cup. I was a coffee snob, drinking only espresso. When a host asked if I'd like coffee, I would say I preferred tea. Now, I was faced with a miserable cup of coffee and a need to be polite. I lifted the mug and tasted. The coffee was rich, strong, and to my liking. I looked up and smiled at Gerhard. This was a good omen. Perhaps, finally, someone would speak with me about *la famille Hirsch*.

"We took contacts," Gerhard said. "Sigismond Hirsch was a good man."

Took contacts. They'd met; they'd spoken. I hadn't expected this close connection. Here was light thrown backward in time. I understood that whatever Gerhard remembered would be story, but wasn't all memory story? I ran my fingers along the fabric of the printed cloth. Perhaps Sigismond had touched this cloth or, if not this one, another like it. Perhaps he'd sat at this table drinking coffee, a fire warming his back. Gerhard unloosed a series of short statements. "Hirsch was an anxious man. He had much culture. He could read Middle High German literature. This was the language of the troubadours." The troubadours composed and performed Old Occitan lyric poetry — Occitan, the archaic language spoken here by a few elders in Auvillar. Occcitan and Middle High German were not the same. I wasn't sure that Gerhard had his facts right.

"He asked me, 'Are you German? When were you born?' I said, 'forty-one.' He replied, 'Ah, that was good you were born then.'"

Born in 1941, Gerhard was too young to have had direct knowledge of the camps, the cattle cars, the daily persecutions. He bore no responsibility for the terrible actions and deeds of his parents' and grandparents' generations. I told Gerhard I was Jewish, that my maiden name was Hirsch, and like Sigismond Hirsch, my family had come from the Alsace-Lorraine. I spoke of my visit to *le mairie* and of my village tour looking for the Hirsch house. I wanted to verify information, so I asked about the house at *numéro trois la place des halles* and of the arrest that took place there.

Gerhard laid both palms firmly on the table. "No, no, the Gestapo did not take them there. They did not live in this village."

I blurted, "That's where they lived. I'm sure of it." I'd peered into the garden at *numéro trois* and I'd pictured them there, *la famille Hirsch*, all taking tea. I'd read Jean Hirsch's testimony on the AJPN website. He spoke of an arrest in Auvillar. On my village tour, the guide had pointed out the house.

Gerhard moved his hands to his knees and sat back. "That would have been impossible. Jews did not live in this village. Auvillar was *judenfrei*. There was a paper the Germans gave."

Judenfrei. Free of Jews. How complete, how utterly and terribly complete. What did the Germans do, go door to door? Take testimony from the mayor and his council? Question the local priest? Gerhard lifted a hand to the back of his neck. "Hirsch was an intellectual. A cultured man. During the war, the family lived in a different village, part of Auvillar, but not the village of Auvillar."

I didn't catch the name of the village. I made a note. "Ask later."

Gerhard spoke of Sigismond and Berthe Hirsch's resistance work organizing transports to save Jewish children. I thought of Kindertransports, passenger trains with Jewish refugee children, their heads turned to watch out windows as these trains slipped from stations, their parents waving frantically from a platform. These trains left Germany and made their way to England, but this was in 1938 and 1939, before actual war had begun.

In describing Sigismond and Berthe's work, the word "transports" was misleading, for the couple saved one or two children at a time, Gerhard said. Working within the organizational structure of the Jewish Scouts, Sigismond Hirsch and other leaders connected their contacts and formed a resistance network that crisscrossed the south of France like a gigantic spider's web. They were logistics consultants and distributors of false documents. They arranged for resistance workers to accompany the children to safe houses or to the Swiss or Spanish borders. They kept apprised of danger, found safer houses, then safer routes. In this way, Sigismond and Berthe Hirsch rescued more than four hundred Jewish children.

I was in awe of their expertise. Their courage. But I was still troubled and wondered again how they could have put their own son in such danger.

"After the parents' arrest, people here in the village hid Hirsch's children," Gerhard said. "Always he was grateful for this."

"Children?"

"There was a girl, a baby named Nicole. She was maybe nine months old. She is troubled."

He said no more. This was what the French called *les non dîtes*, the unspoken, a protected memory.

Sigismond survived the war; Berthe did not, and afterwards, Sigismond reopened his medical clinic in Paris. He returned to Auvillar, bought the house at *numéro trois la place des halles*, and lived there on the occasions he visited Auvillar. Sometimes, he brought Nicole. So Sigismond bought the house in the village *after* the war. "The son is not interested in Auvillar," Gerhard said. "I had him on the phone once. He was not friendly. He told me about his new publication of a book about the Resistance. From what he said, I think he was constructing another vision of himself. He was young. Traumatized."

In his testimony on the AJPN website, Jean Hirsch tells the story of a nine-year-old boy hiding briefly in a convent, then traveling with resistance fighters — first to Cahors, then to Provence where Doctor Daniel, another member of the Resistance, not Jewish, took him in. Jean Hirsch writes of an old ruined farmhouse in the hills at war's end and of seeing American tanks fighting German tanks. He tells of working side by side with Doctor Daniel, bandaging wounds and giving sips of water to the dying. He was not quite twelve at the time and his testimony dates from the vantage point of seventy or so. He describes himself as a liaison officer and then as a caregiver on the battlefield.

After the war, he wandered alone for eighteen months. When I read those words I wondered why, with the networks of resistance workers throughout France, no one had scooped him up and delivered him to Shatta and Simon Boulé, his aunt and uncle, running that safe house in Moissac, a town twelve miles from Auvillar.

Gerhard laced his fingers on the table. "When I was a boy going to school, National Socialism was part of my curriculum. I did not like that part of my education. For me it was not useful to learn that all Germans were criminals. I felt bad about myself. About my country." He gazed at his hands. "Outside of school, Hitler and National Socialism were taboo." After I'd seen those initial images in *Life* magazine and early newsreels I, too, dropped down into silence. Who could talk about such horror? Where was the language?

"These years from 1946 to 1950 were difficult. The first prisoners of war came back. We didn't understand. We did not have enough to eat. The American Army came. They threw away what we did not have. We looked in their garbage," Gerhard said.

It was not until 1968, when social conflicts escalated worldwide and people rebelled against military and bureaucratic elites, that Gerhard said to his parents: "Where were you in 1933?" He was twenty-seven at the time.

I was pleased he'd asked. So many had not.

"We must make a memory of these things that happened, to understand and go on. Humanity has to go on," Gerhard said.

His words were both a statement and a plea. In the States, we mostly have not faced our own dark histories and their legacies: Native American genocide; the internment of the Japanese; and slavery, our greatest and most painful divide.

Gerhard's father was a soldier on the Eastern Front. Gerhard was three, maybe four, when the Allies bombed his family's home in Munich. After the second bombing, he and his mother left for the

Bavarian countryside and the home of his paternal grandparents. Gerhard spoke of a day in April 1945 when the Americans were advancing from the north and German artillery was defending from the south. A grenade exploded near the kitchen. After leaving Munich for safety in the countryside, war had found them again. Gerhard and his aunt were hit by shrapnel, Gerhard's wound superficial, his aunt's severe. At the time, the family was giving refuge to an American soldier. I was not surprised. Earlier, Gerhard had said his mother and father were opposed to Hitler. This was the reason his father had been sent to the Eastern Front, a deployment that was generally a death sentence. In the country house, the American soldier called the Red Cross. An ambulance arrived. As Gerhard waited in the hospital, a nurse handed him an orange. "Never before in my life have I smelled an orange. I will always remember the smell of that orange," Gerhard said.

Perhaps, too, the scent of a war that was finally ending.

At the door, Gerhard handed me a slip of paper with Jean Hirsch's email address.

7

In Valence d'Agen, I seated myself at an outdoor table and ordered two double espressos, one for me, one for Priscilla. This was our plan. I would order coffee; she would bring croissants. The coffee was not good but the location was perfect, tables facing the main square where three fountains sent plumes of water into the air. Today the water was colored blue, not the watery blue of intuition or reflection but cartoon blue. Strange. Why dye water?

As I searched the sidewalk for Priscilla, my mind played tricks. Was I in the right location? Was this indeed the Café Cyrano? No sign on the maroon awning or the door. Had she said nine or ten? Why was my insecurity kicking in? Maybe, I felt troubled about my research. I hadn't yet written to Jean Hirsch. I was uneasy. This was more than my usual angst about approaching a stranger without a connection or an introduction. For years, I'd thought of the *Shoah* as hallowed ground, not a topic I wanted to write about or felt I *could* write about. I asked myself why I felt compelled to do so now.

In the distance I spotted Priscilla walking her bike along the sidewalk and making her way among pedestrians. "Ah, cherie, don't ask. The stupid woman in the pharmacy couldn't find the face cream I was look-ing for, and then the line at the boulangerie — everyone pointing, yes, then no. The damned French can't make up their minds." She ripped open a small wax bag, revealing two crushed golden croissants. "Voilà." I tore a generous hunk. "So, how was dinner last night?" she asked.

She'd angled for an invitation. Wouldn't I ask Cheryl? One more person at the table wouldn't matter. Always, Cheryl cooked in abun-dance. She was sure to have enough. It had been ages, Priscilla said, since she'd spent time with Robert. Naturally she knew he would be there. In this village word traveled. I'd quickly dismissed the idea of inviting her, telling myself this was Cheryl's dinner party, not mine. Truthfully, I didn't want Priscilla at the table, drawing everyone's attention toward her, especially Robert's.

I thought about her affair with Robert and wondered how long it had lasted. Had Robert been her lover before or after the man she called the English bastard? During? In the States, she shared an apartment with a man in Boston, but not on a permanent basis. She also had a man in Virginia. I didn't think he was a lover, but they traveled together. This was the man whose garden she'd designed in Charlottesville planting native species.

Priscilla brushed crumbs from her palms. "You do know that Robert has a girlfriend? The problem is she has a teenaged son."

"I'm not interested in him that way," I said. "Nor is he in me. I've never had an affair, and I'm not going to start now."

"*C'est dommage.*" She gave me a cutting look.

She knew how to push my buttons. When you go through life mar-ried to the same man forever, as I have, you wonder what you might have missed, and if you don't admit to that, you're a liar. I ignored her bait and changed the subject. "So, have you heard of a couple named Sigismond and Berthe Hirsch? They sheltered in Auvillar during the war. The Gestapo arrested them."

"The Gestapo in Auvillar? You're kidding."

"I'm not. They turned their nine-year-old son into a courier for the resistance. He's about seventy-eight now, lives in Paris, and I have his email address, but I'm afraid to contact him. He's a bit of a curmudgeon, I hear. His aunt and uncle ran a safe house in Moissac. That's where we're going, right?"

"A safe house? You mean like for battered women?"

"I mean, for Jewish refugee children. Maybe we can find the house."

"Cherie, people here hated that war. Nobody's going to tell you a thing. Besides, the house is probably long gone. Talk to Robert. He may be Catholic and French, but he's not like the rest of them. He could know something." She stirred her coffee. "You have an address for whats-his-name?"

"Jean Hirsch."

"Why not use it?"

Two days passed before I sifted through email on my computer, clicked the write icon, and typed in Jean Hirsch's address. I wrote of our mutual friend, Gerhard Schneider, and of my interest in his family's history in Auvillar. I pressed send.

That night, I stood at my window and looked out into the night. The air was soft, the moon bright, illuminating the blue suspension bridge and casting ribbons of light on the Garonne. How I loved this village. Ever since I'd read the ex-pats — Hemingway, Gertrude Stein, Alice B. Toklas — I had been drawn to France. It was as if I had tasted France's sunshine, its local wines, its fragrant cheeses long ago. Yet, I hadn't known France's Vichy history. Now, that history called. *The Shoah* called. This period has haunted Jewish American writers from Philp Roth to Nathan Zuckerman, from Cynthia Ozick to Nicole Krauss. Now, this passion was mine.

I boarded the TGV in Agen, a nearby town, and headed for Paris where I was spending a week before heading back to the States. It was the noon hour in Saint Germaine des Prés. I stood outside my hotel on rue de Seine and waited for Valerie. I'd imagined her as dark-haired and elegantly dressed, a scarf tied around her neck. After months of exchanging emails in the virtual world, she and I had not exchanged photos or become friends on Facebook; so I had no idea what she looked like. People rushed past me, men and women, students carrying backpacks, mothers holding the hands of children. Across the street, a florist poured water into buckets of flowers, roses, lilies, iris, daisies, peonies. People exited a boulangerie; they entered restaurants. I searched the crowd. A woman walked up to me. "Sandell?"

The real Valerie was short and plump with a halo of close-cut blonde curls. She wore sand-colored trousers, a sand-colored sweater, and pointy-toed purple suede flats — very Louis XIV. She pulled open a door and stepped inside one of the many bistros lining the street. The maître d' gestured and offered a table on the ground floor near a window, but Valerie asked for one upstairs, and I remembered reading somewhere about the legendary Café de Flore where important and fashionable people shunned tables on the sunny terrace and the ground floor, choosing instead the less pleasant but mostly hidden dining room above. Americans liked to be seen. Parisians preferred to be quietly in-the-know.

At the table, Valerie adjusted her knife, her fork, and her spoon. She lined them up, then ran a palm over the white tablecloth, smoothing wrinkles. These ritual gestures were necessary, it seemed, before she settled back in her chair. "This is better. Yes?"

This upstairs room was empty except for two men dining at a table next to ours. A small dog sat on the floor at their feet. I love that when dining in Paris, dogs are invited to lie beside your table. I leaned over to pet the dog before turning my attention to Valerie.

She smiled and handed me a large glossy menu, the oversized print written in both French and English. This was a tourist menu in a tourist bistro. There were the usual offerings of omelets, salads, an *entrecote* with *pommes frites*. We ordered glasses of white wine and two salads, Valerie's with roasted chicken, mine a *salade niçoise*. I'd adopted the European way of eating, fork in my left hand, knife in my right. I realized all of that switching, right to left, left to right, didn't make sense.

Valerie spoke of her studies in Jerusalem, a time when she'd been interested in the era of the prophets, seers, and charismatic figures who banded together, formed guilds, and passed on their traditions.

Years ago, I'd begun an on-again-off-again journey back to Judaism — mostly intellectual. When I met Lev, a non-traditional rabbi, I joined his synagogue and combined my intellectual pursuits with ritual and spirituality — not God, but something beyond the temporal. At the first service I attended, Lev approached the *bima* or altar, wearing Birkenstocks, a flowing shirt and drawstring trousers, clothes you bought in shops that sold Indian tapestries and beaded necklaces. He was probably in his late twenties, round-faced, portly, charismatic, and he had not yet come out to the congregation, although he was with Andrew, the man he would marry.

Lev did not believe in walls, figurative or real. He dreamed of creating a far-reaching Jewish community that would find its way to our synagogue for retreats and conferences, religious Jews, secular Jews, Reform Jews, Conservative Jews, and non-Jews, all searching for ways to make this world a better place. As a congregation, we failed to help Lev realize his dream, so he left. Yet, he and I remained friends.

During the years I belonged to Lev's congregation, I enrolled in his Introduction to Judaism class and joined his Torah study group. We discussed the Torah portion for the week, talked about Jewish ethics and read Jewish literature, an eclectic mix. I widened my studies and traveled to Hebrew College in Brookline, Massachusetts, for a one-hour class, Discovering Women's Voices in the Bible. There, I uncovered hidden narratives and learned to offer alternatives to male interpretations of women's stories.

❧

"We have nothing like this here," Valerie said. "When I was studying, I thought I would become a professor, but the government assigns these jobs. What if they assigned me to the provinces? I could not bear it."

"You mean you can't choose where you teach?"

She paused, fork and knife mid-air. "France is very closed. It is like being in a box. We say that France is the only place where the Soviet system has succeeded. I became a journalist."

I didn't know what to say, so I nodded. After a pause, I told Valerie that finally I'd from heard Jean Hirsch.

"Yes?"

I twisted slightly in my chair. "I arranged to meet him, then, he cancelled. He told me to read his book."

"So, he will not see you."

I made quotation marks with my fingers. "He's out of town."

"Since you wrote to me, I have tried to think of people I knew who lived through the years of Vichy that I could introduce to you. Tomorrow, I will take you to meet Germaine Poliakov. She is a widow. Her husband was a famous French historian, Léon Poliakov."

Without asking, she did this? I hardly knew her. What did I want with a woman named Germaine Poliakov and her dead husband? What did this woman have to do with my search for Auvillar's Vichy history? Why was Valerie throwing me off track? I glanced at the dog, a rust-colored shaggy-haired fellow lying beside his owner, and smiled. I took a sip of wine and thought about writing.

You followed leads. You didn't know where they would take you. You lived with ambivalence.

"I studied Jewish history with Léon," Valerie said, filling me in. "We became friends. That is how I met her. I had a vague idea of Germaine caring for children during the war, but mostly I thought of her as Léon's wife. I did not realize she had her own story. People came to their flat to interview Léon. Now, you can interview *her*."

I felt inept and unprepared. I was not an experienced interviewer. I hardly knew what questions to ask or how to ask them. My writing was more vague and abstract. My essays appeared in literary journals, not glossy mainstream publications. I set my knife and fork down on my plate. "Valerie, I'm not a journalist."

"Yes, yes, I know. I don't think she understands this. She is ninety-two. I will try to explain. Here writing is different." She went on. "We must take the Metro and the RER."

Did I want to meet this woman? What was the RER? How did it differ from the Metro? Germaine lived in Massy, a suburb south of Paris. Our commute would be an hour. "Tomorrow, I will meet you at Place Saint Michel at eleven. There is a fountain and an angel with wings. Do you know it?"

I did not, but I would.

8

Germaine Poliakov stood in the doorway of her flat, vibrant in her periwinkle blue, V-necked jersey dress. She was extraordinary, mighty, smashing — what the French called *formidable*. Leaning lightly on her cane, she offered her cheek. Now, the other.

In her living room, sunlight streamed through two nearly floor-to-ceiling windows and flooded the room. A narrow balcony held window boxes with pink geranium and trailing ivy. More geranium bloomed in pots. It was mid-October, but in this sun-filled room, the air was summer warm. Germaine's furniture was well-worn, but still elegant: two matching French provincial chairs covered with apricot velvet, and a couch upholstered in muted silk stripes of gray, white, and tangerine. I wondered if, like Germaine, the chairs had survived the war. Could they have been remnants of an earlier life, a life she'd been meant to live?

Potted plants sat on bookcases, window sills, and side tables — peace lilies, ivy, a purple orchid. I, too, grew peace lilies, ivy, and orchids. I presented my gift, a green box tied with a lavender ribbon, macarons from Ladurée, a well-known Parisian pastry shop and tea room. Germaine nodded approvingly. French macarons were not macaroons, those heavy, dense, stringy coconut confections I'd grown up with, served particularly at Passover. Macarons had names like orange blossom, cherry blossom, strawberry, poppy, and they were ambrosia — especially when they came from Ladurée.

Valerie and I took our seats at a round dining table spread with photographs and albums. Germaine hooked her cane over the edge of the table before walking stiffly to the kitchen, a tiny room with an open doorway. I watched as she pulled the lavender ribbon and untied the bow. Now, this ninety-two year-old woman carried a tray with a white porcelain teapot and a white bowl filled with an assortment of macarons and placed it on the table. She returned to the kitchen for an apple tart. "She baked this," Valerie said.

Germaine's flat was a fifth-floor walk-up, and she climbed the stairs twice each day, going out for a walk or to pick up a few things at a grocery. Mostly, the market delivered. "I manage a few small packages," Germaine said.

I pondered my own age. As I grew older, I looked for elder women as beacons. My friend Marie, skiing Vail's back bowls in her late seventies and reading voraciously; my neighbor Jean, in her eighties and wielding a garden spade, also a reader; and now Germaine Poliakov, a French woman who climbed stairs, taught music, and read, too. She held a strainer over a porcelain cup and poured. Valerie and I made room among the photographs for our saucers and cups.

"So, do you have a publisher?" Germaine asked.

The dreaded question, and so early. I shot Valerie a plaintive look. She spoke to Germaine in rapid French, after which Germaine nodded and narrowed her eyes. I read her thoughts, or thought I had. *Who is*

*this woman, this American who has come to take up my time? She is nothing
like the journalists who came to interview Léon.*

"And you want my story?" she said. "Not Léon's?"

"Yes, your story. Perhaps you can start with your family."

Germaine had six sisters and one brother. During the war, one sister
lived in London with her husband. Four sisters, all younger, stayed in
Paris with their mother and their father. Her sister, Josette, like Germaine, was in the south of France. Her brother was in the French Air
Force. Nissim Rousso, Germaine's father, a man who spoke ten languages, had held a high government position in Turkey before emigrating to Paris when Germaine was a toddler. "He was a minister in
the Turkish government," Valerie explained.

I supposed a minister was akin to being a cabinet official in the States.

"My mother was a Cattaui. Do you know the Cattauis?" Germaine
said.

I did not. Valerie filled me in. The Cattaui family were prominent
and prosperous Jewish bankers who had lived in both Austria and
Egypt. In Egypt, they became government administrators, scholars,
scientists, inventors, and dealers in sugar. The family amassed a vast
fortune and Irma, Germaine's mother, a daughter of Fortunée Cattaui, grew up in a seventeen-room palace. The family kept a small
house on the property for a rabbi. Germaine nodded as Valerie spoke.
Although she did not speak English, I felt as if she both understood and
approved Valerie's translation. I eased my way into questions about
Germaine's wartime work, asking first if she remembered the moment
France declared war on Germany. She would have been twenty-one. "I
was with my parents at Le Touquet. We were on the beach when word
came over the loudspeaker. My father said to us, 'Nothing will stop the
Germans.'"

Immediately, the family aborted their holiday and returned to Paris.
Nissim Rousso rented a flat in Brive, a town in the southwest and sent

his family to safety. By June 12, 1940, when the German army crossed the Seine, all of Germaine's family had fled Paris. Nissim, too, had escaped, leaving before the mass exodus with abandoned cars, people fleeing on foot, pulling carts, men and women carrying babies, dragging toddlers, all sharing the clogged roads with France's defeated, demoralized and retreating army. Food and water were scarce. Cars ran out of petrol. Husbands fought with wives, wives with husbands. Babies cried. Children trudged onward. Inns filled beyond capacity. People slept in haylofts and in ditches. They'd waited too long. Not Nissim Rousso.

None of Germaine's family witnessed the first massive flags with swastikas flying from public buildings. None watched as street signs came down, then went up with German names in large text and French names in small text below. None leaned out of windows as German tanks surged on streets or German planes flew overhead. But the expected bombs did not fall. Instead of destroying Paris, Hitler chose to make the city a jewel in his crown. When the Fuhrer's intentions became clear, Germaine's parents and four of her sisters returned to their plush flat near the *Arc de Triomphe*. Germaine and her sister, Josette, remained in the south, although not together.

Speaking of the flat near the *Arc de Triomphe*, Valerie said, "This was a very good address."

In Paris, the *Tricolore* was banned and clocks were turned to Berlin time. A curfew was in effect. The Germans collected all guns. Nissim Rousso did not anticipate what was coming, a Jewish census, a yellow cloth six-pointed Star of David pinned to every Jew's outer garment, even those of children. On the day he was scheduled to register for the Jewish census, Nissim Rousso had a premonition.

Germaine stood. She held a strainer and refilled our tea cups. "My father said to himself, 'This is not such a good idea.' He turned around. Next to him was a Spanish Church. He went inside and talked to a priest. When he came out, he had false Baptism certificates for all of us. This, I refused," Germaine said.

I wasn't sure how word traveled between Paris and Brive, but this was early in the war and German control had not yet tightened. Perhaps by telephone, letter, or telegraph.

"I registered as a Jew," Germaine said.

"Did you wear the yellow star?" I asked.

She shook her head. "No one in the south wore the Star. It was not enforced."

"Your identity card?"

"It said, *Juif*. Not *Juive*. I was upset." The masculine form, not the feminine.

One day, while walking in Brive, Germaine met Madame Rachel Gordin, her old Scout leader, on the sidewalk. Madame Gordin lived in Beaulieu sur Dordogne, a village twenty-five miles south, where she directed *la colonie*, a house that protected Jewish refugee children. Jewish children were pouring out of Germany, Austria, and Poland, if they could. *La colonie* belonged to the Jewish Scouts, the same organization with which Sigismond and Berthe Hirsch were working, all saving Jewish refugee children.

Germaine had not seen her old Scout leader for years. "Come," Madame Gordin said. "Please, I need you to help me manage these girls."

At the table, Germaine popped a bright pink raspberry macaron into her mouth and chewed, mouth open. She swallowed. "I had nothing better to do, so I went."

She turned the page of an album, ran her palm along the open binding, and showed me photos of girls with braids, girls with wild curly hair, all smiling into the camera's lens. These were photos taken at *la colonie*. I used to wear my hair like so many of these girls, parted in the middle and fastened with barrettes. I wore the same dark skirts and white blouses with Peter Pan collars. I belonged to that time, but not to that place. In our living room, war news spilled from the radio. Mama would touch my hair and call me her *shayna maidel*, pretty girl. I understood my blonde hair and blue-green eyes made me special, although I wasn't sure why. Mama said I was safe in America, but I didn't always feel safe. At night I would lie awake in my narrow bed and watch shapes move across the surface of my wall. If I closed my eyes, those shapes glided toward me. In theaters, war movies dragged their images across the screen. I was too young to see those films, but I saw posters. In the yard across the street, I watched older boys play war, shooting and falling down dead.

Germaine took a *nom de guerre* — literally, a name for the war. All the girls knew her as Maki. Only Madame Gordin knew her real name. Her title was *chieftain*, and she worked with three other *chieftains*, sharing a room with Sultan, her best friend, also a *nom de guerre*. Each earned a small salary plus room and board.

"We saved them all," Germaine said, speaking of the girls in *la colonie*, except one. She was homesick and went to her parents in Paris." A long pause. "*Déportée.*"

Deportation meant imprisonment in a French internment camp, probably Drancy on the outskirts of Paris, then a journey east in a cattle car and almost certain death. As Germaine lowered her gaze, I placed my tea cup noiselessly into the ring of my saucer offering a few seconds of silence for that dead child.

Germaine spoke of combing lice from the girls' hair twice each day and mending their clothes. I had expected to hear tales of harrowing escapes, of near captures, of slick moves, of life so heightened the hairs on the back of her neck bristled, not a tale of combing lice. Germaine cooked. She gave lessons. She was a musician, voice her instrument.

Before the war, she was studying at the Music Academy of Paris and singing in a trio with two of her sisters, Germaine the bass. They won a contest, their prize a spot to sing on the radio, but they could not collect. By then, the Nazis had taken over. No Jews on the radio. In Beaulieu sur Dordogne, Germaine formed a choir and taught the girls Hebrew melodies she'd learned years before when she was a Scout and Madame Gordin was her leader. Abruptly, Germaine lifted her chin, "There is nothing more to tell you. My life was ordinary. Nothing special."

Was she ending our interview? I lifted my hand and touched the border of a photograph. "You?"

"*Oui.*"

In the photo, Germaine is a tall, full figured woman with broad shoulders and dark wavy hair that frames her face. She stands in front of a car with the three other *chieftains*. They link arms. Germaine is not beautiful, but she has a certain allure. She gazes sideways at the camera.

Now, seeing herself young, Germaine's own gaze lingered. I pointed to a photo of two women and three men sitting on a bench inside a walled courtyard. The men wore berets and *tallit*, prayer shawls, and held prayer books. "They are studying Torah with Leo Cohn," Germaine said.

I looked up. "That was unusual, men and women studying Torah side by side."

"Not for him," Germaine said.

"Did you study?"

"I am secular."

Germaine spoke of Leo Cohn — Zionist, Jewish scholar, educator, and accomplished musician. He played piano and flute, and when he visited *la colonie*, he and Germaine sang duets. Cohn traveled throughout France, visiting the Scouts' network of safe houses and teaching Torah. He was worried about France's Jews. So many were secular, and like Germaine, they had little or no knowledge of Torah. Although Germaine did not share Cohn's Zionist or religious views, she adored him.

In his travels, Leo Cohn distributed false identity papers and escorted small groups of Jewish children across Swiss and Spanish borders. Fearless, he boarded trains in cities and towns where the Gestapo hunted him, and under his guidance five hundred Jewish children reached safety. On May 17, 1944, in the Toulouse railroad station, his luck ran out. The Gestapo arrested him. Germaine's gaze lingered on his face. Slowly and softy she uttered that single word. "*Déporté*."

Leo Cohn, a man with a prominent nose, a receding hairline, and wearing glasses, bore an uncanny resemblance to my father.

As Germaine flipped pages and pointed to young men, she spoke that single word again and again: "*Déporté*."

I wondered about *la colonie*. I pictured a stone farmhouse with a red-tiled roof like the farmhouse at the crest of the hill I passed on my daily walks in Auvillar. Perhaps, though, *la colonie* sat at the end of a long dirt drive, only its roof visible. Inside, Germaine taught the girls math, history, and geography. She led the girls in song. I understood that in those moments of lessons and song, war seemed far away. Perhaps that was what Germaine meant when she said life was ordinary.

What of life outside? In the album there are photos of girls at the river in Beaulieu sur Dordogne. Did they walk to the river, stop in a boulangerie to buy baguettes? Did they pass German soldiers? In times of war, rumors spread like seeds on the wind. Fear floated. Germaine's family was far away, their fate unknown. Only Josette was nearby. And what of these girls, these young refugee girls living in *la colonie*, some orphaned, some with parents in prison or in hiding, none knowing, all hoping their parents, their sisters, their brothers, their cousins, their aunts, their uncles, and their friends were safe, but suspecting they weren't, all relying on Madame Gordin, Germaine, and the other *chieftains* to keep them out of harm's way?

Could the house have been a meeting place of the resistance where young fighters, men and women, stood at the door? In my musings, it was night, someone knocked, and Germaine opened the door a crack to peer out. Three, four, five resistance fighters entered the house, bringing with them the scent of danger, the exhilaration of escape. I saw bottles of wine and beer on a kitchen table. Someone laughed, and someone else whispered, "Shhh, you'll wake the girls."

In Germaine's flat, I looked out a window and beyond the narrow balcony with its blooming pots of pink geranium. Leaves on trees shimmered yellow in the light. I had so many questions. What did she know of battles and bombings? Of mass arrests throughout Europe? Had she seen planes overhead? And who was she to the villagers, a Jew in hiding? A refugee? I said, "So *la colonie* was run by the Jewish Scouts, and the Scouts were part of the resistance, so I suppose that would make you part of the resistance, too. Did you think of yourself that way?"

Germaine straightened her spine. She spoke to Valerie in rapid French, and as she spoke, she did not take her eyes from my face. "*Pourquoi est-elle si intéressée par ce sujet?*"

I understood every word. Why was I so interested in this subject? I'd touched an old tender wound. What was it? Perhaps if I shared my own thoughts she would share hers. "I was very young during the war, but I have memories," I said. "At night a man used to walk past our house and call, 'Lights out, lights out.' He worked for the Civil Defense. We were afraid of enemy planes." I spoke of visiting Grandma Rose and Grandpa Harry, my father's mother and step-father, at the Jersey Shore. Dad would stand on the Boardwalk in Asbury Park and point to the horizon, a forlorn look on his face. "They spotted a U-boat out there." We were Jews, and we knew, if not specifically, then inherently, what that meant to our distant and unknown cousins across the sea.

Germaine's body softened. "I did not know you thought about the war in America."

How could she not have known? Then I thought of all I did not know about her. I pointed to a portrait on a wall. In the painting, a man sits in one of the apricot velvet chairs, holding his hands as if in prayer and pressing his long index fingers to his lips. He is a thin man with a long face, a narrow nose, and contemplative eyes. "Léon?" I said.

"Léon," she answered.

"Did you meet him in Beaulieu sur Dordogne?"

Germaine turned to Valerie. "She does not want to speak about this," Valerie said. "She wants to know if you have heard of Rabbi Zalman Chneerson?" Valerie wrote the name on a slip of paper, Chneerson spelled with a C, not an S. I was familiar with Schneerson, an ultra-Orthodox rabbi in Brooklyn, but this was not the same person.

"Léon worked with Chneerson," Germaine said.

A diversion, but what could I do?

"This was unusual," Valerie said, "a secular Jew and an Orthodox rabbi working together."

Germaine launched into her story. Léon and the rabbi arrived in Nice with a group of Jewish children, when suddenly the Nazis were everywhere. *Nice.* Not *Beaulieu sur Dordogne.* They could not stay. Somehow, Léon procured a truck, but the truck had an open back. Léon collected cardboard boxes and hid the children under the cardboard. He and Chneerson drove the children from Nice to safe houses in the countryside, dropping them off one by one. This was a wireless network of communication working by word of mouth, courier, instinct, courage, and luck. Poliakov and Chneerson returned to Nice and hid out in a vacant flat.

"They had nothing to eat," Germaine said, "so Léon went out to buy food. The *rebbe* said, 'Not this food. It is not kosher.' Also, it was Yom Kippur, and Chneerson wanted to blow the *shofar*."

The *shofar* is an instrument made from a ram's horn, and when you blow, the sound blasts louder than a trumpet.

"Léon said to Chneerson, 'There is no way you can blow the *shofar*.'

'Chneerson said, 'On Yom Kippur I blow the *shofar*.'

'Léon said, 'Wait. Promise you'll wait until I return.'

"Léon went to the railroad station and he checked the..."

Translating, Valerie gestured. "How do you say in English *horaire*?"

I shook my head.

Valerie pursed her lips and continued to translate Germaine's words. "Léon went back to the flat. He showed the *rebbe* this paper."

Suddenly, I understood. "Timetable."

"Timetable?"

"Schedule for the trains."

"Ah," Valerie said. "Léon said to the rebbe, 'You can blow the *shofar* here and here.' So, when the train went past, Chneerson blew."

A story of Léon's cleverness, his triumph. This was what Germaine wanted to show me; yet, this story was so much more, touching as it did on an essential question: What did it mean to be a Jew? For some the *shofar* must sound. For others, like Léon, silence worked. For me, the question was an ongoing search.

I still didn't know how or when Germaine met Léon.

In his essay "The Meaning of Homeland," Amos Oz, an Israeli writer who was not religious — no revelation, no faith — wrote, "I am a Jew and a Zionist." According to Oz, a Jew is a person who calls herself or himself a Jew, or one who others force to be a Jew. He wrote:

"A Jew, in my unhalachic opinion, is someone who chooses to share the fate of other Jews, or who is *condemned* to do so."

Unhalachic, not according to the law.

❧

One night in 1998, leaving a movie theater with Dick, I was furious. We had just seen Roberto Benigni's award-winning film *Life is Beautiful*. At the end of the war, when the Americans are near, the death camp pictured in the film breaks into chaos. Guido, the main character, played by Benigni, hides Giosue, his son, in a sweatbox, explaining that this is the final move in a game the two have been playing for years. Guido disappears. When finally, the Americans liberate the camp, Giosue climbs out of the sweat box. There he is, a small boy, facing a gigantic American tank, the prize his father has promised. Giosue has won the game.

Sitting in the car after the movie, I yanked my seatbelt across my lap. "How could he do that, make a comedy about the Holocaust? Nobody won that game. Not the dead, not the survivors."

For years we couldn't talk about what had happened. For years those murders had no name. The Holocaust wasn't a game.

Dick backed out of our parking space, his face calm. This was what my anger did to him — sent him into a silence that looked like ease. He shifted the car into drive. "Maybe there's another way to look at the film," he said.

"There isn't. There can't be. There is no way Guido would have gotten away with all he did. There's no way that child would have survived. And what of the other children, the ones who arrived with Giosue? Where is Benigni on them?"

"It's not real," Dick said.

"That's the point."

"You're right. That *is* the point."

I sulked all the way home, refusing to suspend belief, my feelings raw and visceral.

Germaine lowered her gaze. "I met a young man, Ralph Weyl. He was a resistance fighter, very handsome. He lived seventeen kilometers from Beaulieu. We married. He wasn't — how do you say — very nice. He found others. I had three children."

She recited their names, Daniel, Aline, and Arlette. These children were my contemporaries.

Germaine whispered. "He left me."

I wanted to touch her arm and ease her painful memory, but we were not yet friends and I didn't know the customs here. Above all, I didn't want to offend. I mulled her words — married to a resistance fighter who was not Léon, a man who returned from missions smelling of danger and other women, a man who impregnated her three times and, after the war, left for good.

In the summer of 1942 and into the fall of 1943, Hitler intensified his war against the Jews. He gave the French quotas for deportations and, because of the Jewish census taken early in the war, officials had the names and addresses of all Jews. Germaine spoke of sewing money and letters into the hems of the girls' skirts. If found or rescued, each could be identified. Beaulieu sur Dordogne had either been a strategic or a lucky choice for a safe house, probably a little of each. Notices of impending roundups went to the gendarmerie in advance. French officers needed time to procure vehicles and have the necessary personnel available. In Beaulieu, one gendarme, Amédée Duhaut, warned Madame Gordin of scheduled roundups. She emptied the house. She, the *chieftains*, and the girls marched and followed paths in the woods.

Being scouts with wilderness skills, they pitched tents. Mornings, they broke camp and moved on, and so it went until danger had passed. Germaine called these "flying camps."

An iconic saga, a safe house no longer safe, money sewn into hems, girls hiding in a forest, and now that story was here in this Parisian living room. I had never known war, and in spite of movies and my father's ominous warnings as he pointed out to sea, I could not truly imagine war, the fear, the hunger, the disruption, the loss, lives changing instantaneously.

Germaine said, "I do not believe the children suffered or were sad. When they went to sleep at night, they asked me to kiss. So, I kissed."

I asked about a single day Germaine remembered vividly. Germaine folded her hands loosely in her lap and spoke of a day in 1944 when German soldiers were marching though Beaulieu sur Dordogne and heading to Normandy. They were nervous, edgy, and shooting wildly. "I was..." Germaine rounded her hands and drew a dome in front of her belly... "expecting my third child, carrying my baby in one arm, dragging Daniel by his hand and running across a field to the woods. I heard a shot. I knew what it was. I wasn't frightened. I felt calm. I don't know why."

Naturally she was frightened. But fear propelled her and gave her strength, a pregnant woman carrying her baby, dragging her toddler, her heart pounding, her belly cramping, adrenaline pumping her legs.

I looked into my cup of golden tea. How did she find her way through all that, then integrate into the person she had become?

A few days before, Germaine's granddaughter, a woman who became very religious and lived in Israel, had come to visit with her children, boys who wore *peyes*, side curls. "I wanted to make them lunch," Germaine said. "They came from so far. I offered a cup of tea.

My granddaughter refused. She would not let the boys eat, not even a cookie." This woman was the daughter of the baby in Germaine's belly that day she raced for the woods. "I knew they were Orthodox. Still, I was insulted. I don't like Orthodox."

She meant Orthodoxy. I agreed. Had I been visiting that day, I would have told that granddaughter to forget her rules of *kashrut* that allowed her to eat only kosher foods from kosher plates and to drink only from kosher cups. I would have told her to take a cup of tea with her grandmother, to let Germaine give cookies to the boys. Their great-grandmother had been to the edge and survived. To break bread, to share a meal with family and friends, this was *naches*, a Yiddish word that, like most Yiddish words, squiggled out from under definition. *Naches* was pleasure, but more than pleasure. *Naches* was the pure joy a child brought to a parent or grandparent.

Speaking English, Germaine said, "The more and more I get old, the more I can express what I feel. Only now, I realize my life was not ordinary."

So, we agreed.

At the door, Germaine said, "People tell me I was courageous to do what I did. I did not know."

Perhaps courage is acting, not out of bravery, but out of the essence of who you are.

Germaine offered her cheek, and we kiss-kissed. She was tired. She must nap. We'd talked a long time. "You are going back to the States?" she said.

"Yes," I said. I'd been away a month. I had decided, with fairness to Dick, a month was the limit for my absences. For years, he provided the financial and emotional support for me to become more than I ever thought I could be, and I was grateful.

Germaine and I exchanged email addresses. She took my hand and held on. "You must tell me when will you return." Not if I would return. When. I thought about journalists coming to interview Léon, but never Germaine as she sat in one of the apricot velvet chairs, looking on, her own story rumbling in her belly. Yes, I would return to listen to Germaine and continue my search for answers to questions I hardly knew. The best way to find what I was looking for was: let it reveal itself.

9

At home, I read as much about Vichy France as I could find. Germaine and I exchanged emails. Valerie and I exchanged emails. I tested my notes and my memory against Valerie's memory. She suggested books and I read them: *The Imaginary Jew*, by Alain Finkielkraut; an old guidebook; *Paris Judaica*, by Emmanuel Haymann De Noel. In return, I read documents related to her work with Thierry that she had translated into English, and corrected her grammar and word choice. All of our friendships deepened, mine and Valerie's, mine and Germaine's, and by spring of the following year, I was planning my return. In 2013, I returned both spring and fall, leaving behind my expanded household — husband, son, granddaughter, and dogs. I have always loved the chase and the hunt, that determination of pursuit even when what I'm chasing is not in sight. I rarely give up. In that sense, I am my father's daughter. "Quitters never win, and winners never quit," he would say.

That May, Germaine asked if I'd like to meet one of the girls she'd cared for in *la colonie*. Meet a child who had lived in *la colonie*? I hadn't dreamed of the possibility.

Valerie accompanied me to translate. She had met Yvonne years before, and as we traveled on the Metro, she filled me in on Yvonne's story. Now eighty-four, Yvonne lived in the Nineteenth Arrondissement, a district with a large and mostly observant Jewish population. She, too, was observant, keeping kosher, conservative, but she bent certain rules. Although Yvonne blessed the candles, observed *shabbat*, and celebrated all Jewish holidays, she also cared for and walked her neighbor's dog on the sabbath. One time, Valerie said, a religious Jew stopped her on the sidewalk and scolded her. "What," she said to the man, "you don't pee on *shabbat*?"

I liked her already.

Yvonne lived in a pre-war building with a small cage-like elevator barely large enough for the two of us. We rode in near darkness up through the interior of the building, machinery groaning. Yvonne waited in an open doorway. She was a diminutive woman with a dowager's hump, and she moved as Germaine moved, quickly and with purpose, walking now to her kitchen, then back, carrying first a pot with tea, then a plate with *nonettes*, jam-filled cakes named for the nuns who used to make them. She set the plate on the table and poured tea. The only window in this room looked out on the Parc des Buttes-Chaumont across the road. I was eye level with leafy crowns of century-old chestnut trees. Far below, traffic passed noiselessly on a busy street. This flat was nothing like Germaine's bright space. No orchids. No geranium. No sun.

I was surprised to learn that Yvonne was German, surprised, too, that neither Germaine nor Valerie had told me this. I'd assumed she was a French child sent to the south for safety. Turned out Yvonne was born in Mannheim, a city across the Rhine River from Ludwigshafen, the city where she lived until she was nine. Her given name was Inga Sigrid

Borhmann, and her family — both sides — had lived in Ludwigshafen for ten generations, firmly rooted in German soil. Yvonne's grandfather and father, Ernst Bohrmann, traded in carriage horses. She'd expected that she, too, would grow up in Ludwigshafen, but the Nazis had had other ideas.

Yvonne fingered a honey-brown gemstone at her neck and spoke to me of *Kristallnacht* and the burning synagogue, her father rushing out of their flat and racing to rescue *tallit*, prayer shawls, and *sidur*, prayer books. I'd never been this close to someone who'd experienced that night, the acrid smell of burning buildings, the sounds of storefront windows shattering, the shouts of gangs in the street beating Jews, the cries of terror. Still, her father had run out into the tumult to rescue Torahs and *tallit*. Yvonne said, "My father returned. He carried *tallit*. Police came and took him away. Thugs came. They tore pictures from the walls and threw them into the street."

She spoke in short, simple sentences, reducing memory to simple facts devoid of emotion, perhaps because the child who had once lived inside of her was beyond her recognition or held so tightly that she remained hidden. I wasn't sure which came first, the thugs or the arrest. Had Yvonne, her sister Marion, and Else, their mother, stayed in the flat and watched? Or had they sought refuge with a neighbor? How long did the rioting last? How long did the thugs stay in the flat? Yvonne shook her head. She did not know. She laced her fingers on the table, unlaced, and laced again. "They took all of the Jewish men that night. Later, I heard them singing, 'Did you see the little *kohn* with big ears like a donkey's?'"

Kohn. Jew.

She remembered the lyrics of a song that stigmatized, punished, and shamed. She did not remember details of the horror. She stared at a small-screened television, rabbit ears perched on top. "The day after, I saw the shops. The broken windows. The burned synagogue."

Here in this flat, my belly hollowed out. I could not fathom seeing police take my father away or thugs filling my living room. What had this done to this child?

Yvonne remembered a dream. "I had a doll. You could turn the arms and legs. I took the doll and I threw it away in the cement yard. The doll broke, then came on fire. I was very angry."

I saw the doll landing, body, head, arms, and legs smashing, then rising in flames. All through the war, Yvonne dreamed that dream. Now, leaning an elbow on the table, Yvonne said, "I wonder what that doll symbolized."

Life as she and her family had known it for generations began its end in 1933 when Hitler came to power. On *Kristallnacht*, it was finished.

Nearly seven weeks after his arrest, Ernst Borhmann returned from Dachau and knocked on the door of his own flat. For reasons no one knew, the Germans had released him. The next morning, Else dressed her daughters in layers of clothing — underwear, skirts, blouses, sweaters, socks. Gloves and a hat. Baggy leggings. Perhaps matching coats of good wool, coarse to the touch and softened with velvet collars, the style in 1938, wool and velvet. Yvonne was nine, Marion twelve, and at that moment Yvonne was still known as Inga.

Yvonne remembered events and feelings. She did not remember details, so I conjured them, baggy leggings, coats with velvet collars. Yvonne did remember a brown leather satchel, small and shaped like an envelope, hanging low below her hip bone. In it she'd packed paper, pencils for drawing, a little money, and a trinket or two. She also carried a small valise, as did Marion. Yvonne was still Inga. I saw her standing outside the building where she lived, adjusting the strap of her brown leather satchel and looking longingly up at a window framing her mother's face.

I imagined a sky hanging low, snow drifting down, Inga lifting her chin and darting her tongue to taste. She was a curious child but, at this moment, subdued. All her life she had known only Hitler and anti-Semitism — Jewish doctors forbidden to practice, Jewish teachers dismissed from their jobs, Jewish shops boycotted and then closed, Jewish graves desecrated. Silently she'd watched her world shrink, absorbing as a child absorbed, seeing, hearing, touching. Forbidden to attend her German school, she was sent to a Jewish school where fifty children learned with one teacher. She didn't like the press of so many bodies. Often, she could not hear the teacher's voice. Always, there were new laws against Jews. One day, walking with her mother, she saw a marquee announcing a Shirley Temple film. She loved Shirley Temple. "Why, *Mutter*, why can't I go inside?"

Ernst had wanted all of the family to emigrate to the States, but he had not been able to find a way. On that snowy December day, he was sending Inga and Marion to live with his sister, Toni, in Strasbourg, France. He rode with them on a train as far as Kehl, walked with them to a bridge that crossed the Rhine. Inga looked up at her father. "When will you come?"

"Later."

"And *Mutter*?"

"Later, too."

In Strasbourg, the girls stayed with Aunt Toni for a night, but she was a widow and could not afford to keep them. Did Ernst know that when he watched his daughters walk across the bridge his sister had had other plans for his girls? The next morning, Inga stood on a platform beside Aunt Toni and watched as Marion boarded a train bound for Paris, where she would stay with Lisolotte, a cousin, recently married. Inga wanted to go to Paris, too. She'd never seen Paris. Why couldn't she go? Why couldn't she stay with Lisolotte? Why only Marion? How easily I inserted my own longing here — I, the child who tugged at her father's trouser leg and whined, "Why, Daddy, why? Why can't I go?"

Aunt Toni and Inga boarded a different train, one bound for Sarreg-uemines, a city sixty-two miles north, on the Saar River. There, Inga would stay with Aunt Marthe, sister to both Aunt Toni and Ernst. Like Aunt Toni, Aunt Marthe had married a French citizen, Maurice Samu-els, and this, the family believed, would keep Inga safe. Proprietors of a shirt factory, the family was wealthy. They had no children. On the train, Aunt Toni whispered, "You will live in a big house. Your Aunt Marthe will buy you pretty frocks."

Inga hardly knew Aunt Marthe and Uncle Maurice. She did not want pretty frocks. She wanted to go to Paris. She wanted Marion. She wanted her parents.

I imagined Inga on that train, a brown-haired child with brown eyes, one larger than the other, hunkering down and turning her whole body to the window. Winter moved toward her, the frozen ground, the metal gray sky. She felt as if she were entering a tunnel. Where was the end? She clutched her brown leather satchel and stroked the leather as if it were a dog's furry coat.

In Sarreguemines, children attended either a Protestant or a Cath-olic school. This pleased Inga. She'd had a friend in Ludwigshafen, a girl who belonged to the Hitler Youth. Let's call her Ursula. After coming home and changing out of her uniform, Ursula knocked on Inga's door, and even though she could have gotten into big trouble, she played with Inga. Inga hoped that, in the Protestant school Aunt Marthe had chosen, she would find a friend like Ursula. On her first day, Inga sat at her desk, words swarming like bees. She didn't understand, not a word. She bowed her dizzy head. Her teacher spoke French, only French. Inga spoke only German. Her teacher gave her a new name. She was no longer Inga; she was Yvonne. She felt like an orphan.

Sarreguemines was in the Alsace, and when Hitler took over the Alsace-Lorraine region, he expelled the Jews and confiscated their property. Germans took the Samuels' home and their shirt factory.

103

Yvonne fled south with her aunt and her uncle. At the same time, Lisolotte and Marion were leaving Paris and also traveling south to Beaulieu sur Dordogne, where Lisolotte would briefly direct *la colonie* before following her husband to the States. Madame Gordin would become the second director of *la colonie*. After months of travel without a destination, Aunt Marthe and Uncle Maurice left Yvonne at *la colonie* and went into hiding nearby.

At the table, Yvonne reached for her porcelain tea cup. "I liked very much living with the other girls, but at night I cried. I spoke German. I did not like speaking French. Maki scolded. (Maki, Germaine.) She said I must speak French, only French. And without my German accent. If I did not listen, I would get us all arrested. Maki was tough. Nice, but tough." She set her cup down into the ring in her saucer without drinking. "I wanted very much to sing in Maki's choir. She did not want me to sing. I had a very deep voice. Not soprano."

I remembered a photograph in *The History of Beaulieu Sur Dordogne*, the book Germaine had shown me — girls standing in a plaza in front of *la colonie*, arms outstretched to form a six-pointed Star of David. This was early in the war, before the pervasive presence of German soldiers and increased Vichy propaganda had turned most of the populace in the south against Jews. In the photograph, Maki stood off to one side, arms raised and ready to give the downbeat. The girls sang *Ma Tovu*, a Hebrew prayer, Maki announcing that *Ma Tovu* was an "oriental" melody. Yvonne knew *Ma Tovu*, every note and every word. She used to sing it in Ludwigshafen on Yom Kippur, the Day of Atonement, the holiest day of the Jewish year. To this day, Yvonne remembered Maki's words, so deep was her hurt and her desire. "She said to me, 'You will spoil the sound.'"

Growing up under Hitler, Yvonne was marked. Now, at *la colonie*, she was flawed in a different way. How isolated she must have felt. Still, Yvonne loved Maki, and continues to love her.

☙

At home in the States, I'd read of Hitler's order to evacuate all Jews from the German states of Baden, the Palatinate, and Württemberg. Cattle cars waited at train stations. Ludwigshafen was in the Palatinate, and Ernst and Else Bohrmann were among those arrested and deported. France had a network of internment camps, some created during the First World War and others built for Spanish refugees fleeing the Spanish Civil War. One of them, Gurs, sat in the foothills of the Pyrenees close to the Spanish border, and that was where the train carrying Ernst and Else Bohrmann discharged its human cargo.

Gurs was an internment camp, not a concentration camp; still, conditions were harsh. Frigid air penetrated the women's and the men's barracks. Blankets were thin, rations sparse. Prisoners starved. They needed medicine and potable water. A guard would heave a single loaf of bread into a barracks of thirty women, who would attack the loaf like the animals they had become. Outside, the mud was so deep that one night, on the way to the latrine, a woman drowned. Others died of typhoid fever or dysentery. Ever since his imprisonment in Dachau, Ernst's lungs were bad. In Gurs, they worsened.

Not many prisoners left Gurs with their freedom. Most were shipped to Drancy. But Lisolotte, working with the Red Cross before leaving France, had obtained their release: Ernst and Else Bohrmann made their way to *la colonie*.

☙

In her flat all these years later, Yvonne lowered the plate of *nonettes* to the table. With an index finger she slowly traced a flower on the plastic tablecloth. "What was difficult when my parents came to Beaulieu from Gurs," she said. "I felt like they were not my parents. I looked at them. I did not know them. They were…" She searched for a word. "Sedated."

Quiet, blunted, and broken in ways a child could not name.

"They had lost weight. They were old. I was living in a community of girls. That was my life. I called Maki *ma mère*."

Then and now, Yvonne was not ashamed of her behavior. She was a child and she was angry. I understood. I would have felt and acted the same way.

Her mother, her father, Aunt Toni, Aunt Marthe, Uncle Maurice, and another uncle, all sheltered in basement rooms near the river in Beaulieu sur Dordogne. Her parents wanted Yvonne to live with them, but she refused. The Borhmanns and Madame Gordin reached a compromise: Yvonne would spend her days learning her lessons, doing her chores, and eating her meals with Maki and the girls. Nights, she'd sleep in her family's dark basement rooms.

One day, Uncle Maurice walked to the gendarmerie and asked to see Monsieur Duhaut, the friendly gendarme. Maurice wanted to travel to Brive. Was that possible? Duhaut pulled a paper from a pile. "Look at this list. Tomorrow morning, soldiers and police are coming with buses to arrest all the names here."

He saw his name, his wife's name, his brother-in-law's name, his sister-in-law's name, and Yvonne's parents' names, along with the names of certain girls in *la colonie*. The family scattered. Madame Gordin emptied the house. Rucksacks on their backs, the girls, including Yvonne, left the village and marched into the countryside to set up camp. Day after day, they moved on until danger passed. The girls whose names were not on the list returned to *la colonie*. The others traveled to safe houses or to convents, escorted by members of the Resistance.

In the fall of 1942, following the British and American landings in Morocco and Algeria, the Wehrmacht entered the southern zone. Before that there had been a strong German presence, along with a pretense of French governance. Now, that pretense was gone. The Germans stepped up raids and deportations. Beaulieu sur Dordogne was no longer safe. Still, the Scouts did not close the doors of *la colonie* until December 1943. One by one, resistance workers escorted each of the girls to safety. Claude Samuels, a resistance worker and Yvonne's cousin, took her to a convent in Tulle, a village twenty miles north. Marion, three years older, was dropped at the Swiss border and told to make her way. The rest of the family quit their basement flat and scattered.

"When Claude left me with the nuns in Tulle, he did not say I was Jewish," Yvonne said.

I pictured her, fourteen, standing in an entryway, a large wooden door closing behind her. Her parents were gone. Marion was gone. Maki was gone, and Claude, too, was gone, sucked up into the night. She fingered the strap of her brown leather satchel.

Yvonne said, "Suddenly, I was a Catholic orphan. I did not want to put my fingers in the Holy water. On the day of Confession, I said I was sick. On Yom Kippur, I had a headache; I must stay in bed. A girl brought me food. I placed the food in a cupboard and waited for night."

Yom Kippur was a fast day. Perhaps Yvonne clung to ritual as if to transcend time, remembering holidays in Ludwigshafen when the family would gather — grandparents, aunts, uncles, cousins, her mother, her father, her sister. I thought of the yellow stucco house and Jewish holiday dinners with Mama and Papa and all of the family. No one argued, not even my father. Peace hovered over the table like mist. Perhaps, too, Yvonne thought of Marion, walking paths in a Swiss forest with no one to guide her. Did Marion know which day was Yom Kippur? Did she need to know?

One morning, without notice or explanation, the nuns sent Yvonne to a new school. "I was sitting next to a girl I knew in Beaulieu, the daughter of a grocer. She knew I was Jewish. I was worried. I sent word to Claude."

Soon, Yvonne was traveling again, this time to a convent in Saint Etienne, a city near Lyon, about a hundred and ninety miles east. "Here the nuns knew I was Jewish. They tried to convert me," Yvonne said.

I could envision a small room with stone walls, a chair where Yvonne sat. Another chair where a nun sat. The nun was not unkind, but she was austere, her face narrowed by her wimple. She was afraid for Yvonne. If Yvonne did not believe in the Savior, she would burn in hell. Perhaps at that moment Yvonne remembered Kristallnacht, and the dream of her porcelain doll shattering, then rising in flames. No, Yvonne would not burn in hell. She did not believe in hell.

Yvonne said, "In a house near this convent, a priest was hiding three Jewish boys and teaching them *Torah*. He was preparing them to make their bar mitzvahs after the War."

This was the complexity of that time, a nun who wanted to convert a Jewish child, a priest who taught three Jewish boys *Torah*.

Yvonne spoke of the spring of 1944 when everyone who could get near a clandestine radio listened to the BBC. The Royal Air Force and American B-17's were bombing Berlin. The family, Yvonne, her mother, her father, her aunts — all except Marion, who was in Switzerland, and Uncle Maurice, who would die or had already died in Auschwitz — came together in Vabre, a village in Tarn in the southeast. Who, Maurice had wondered, would arrest a sixty-two year-old man? This despite the fact that he'd seen his name on a list, earlier. Perhaps he was tired of running.

In Vabre, the men joined the Protestant Maquis, a resistance fighting group, and the family, nine in all, hid in a house next to a Protestant church. Yvonne said, "When the Germans came, one of the men placed a ladder across the open space between the two roofs. I crawled across."

"You crawled across?" I said, trying to imagine myself on my hands and knees, my arm reaching for the next rung, a deep emptiness below.

Yvonne smiled. "I did not look down."

In the dark cavernous church, hiding was easy.

From somewhere in this building, a dog barked. Her neighbor's dog, the dog she cared for. Searching under the table with her toes, Yvonne slipped her stocking feet into a pair of brown leather flats. "I must take him out." Valerie and I stood. We took our leave. Outside on the sidewalk, we stood in silence for a moment, each of us pondering Yvonne's story. Blossoms from the flowering chestnut trees drifted like snow, and I conjured an image of two girls from long ago, sisters walking to the train station with their father on a cold, snowy December day.

In a courtyard of the *Mémorial de la Shoah*, I walked slowly around a large brass cylinder that evoked a chimney. Raised letters on the circumference spelled out Belzec, Buchenwald, Chelmno, Dachau, Majdanek, Maluthausin, Sobibor, Struthof, Treblinka, Auschwitz, Bergen-Belsen, Warsaw Ghetto. Words both familiar and strange, places few people remembered directly, Yvonne and Germaine two of the last living links to that time. During the war years when she cared for children in *la colonie*, Germaine claimed she had no knowledge of the camps. "Only Madame Gordin, who had been to Germany, knew," she said. The phrase intrigued me — *been to Germany*. Perhaps Madame Gordin had witnessed the early racial laws, as Yvonne had. Perhaps she'd understood hatred in a way that others had not. Yvonne was too young to have known of the camps. Yet, this larger story of deportation and murder that played out without their knowledge gave their lives context. Without both the larger story and the individual story, the *I* disappeared. I thought of *Bloodlands*, Timothy Snyder's history of mass killings, the larger story, and of those folded notes thrown from cattle cars, the individual story.

All of us, Jews and non-Jews, belonged to that larger story. Yet, as Jews, we needed to be careful. How tempting to some to take their identity from the camps as if to reduce our grand culture of religious scholarship, literature, philosophy, mathematics, ritual, and spirituality — to genocide. Folks who did that saw an anti-Semite around every corner. In order to discover who we are, we need to dig under those years of horror and under our fear. Our stories, collective or individual, do not begin with that time any more than my story begins with my paternal great-grandparents who washed up on American shores. A writing residency drew me to Auvillar. Curiosity drew me to Lev and questions about Auvillar's Vichy history. Events followed, my discovery of Jean Hirsch and our matching last names, Lev's introduction to Valerie, Valerie's introduction to Germaine, Germaine's to Yvonne, and I spiraled down into all of their stories, connecting myself to the larger story of my heritage.

⫷

The courtyard of the *Mémorial de la Shoah* was large, flanked by two stone walls with benches flush to each of them. I sat on a bench and breathed deeply. I let out air in a slow release, as if to empty the sadness inside. On the stone wall across the courtyard I noticed sculptures in relief. I rose and walked toward them. I read a plaque. These were bas reliefs sculpted by Arbit Blatas, a Lithuanian-born artist whose career bridged Venice, New York and Paris. He had escaped the Nazis in 1941 and fled to the States. The reliefs are scenes of persecutions. In one,

110

three soldiers aim their rifles at a woman standing against a wall. Off to one side, a soldier holds the next victim. These reliefs are an assembly line of terror and death, and although the images are of stone, they have the characteristics of sketches, giving the impression that they are both solid and ephemeral — like memory.

In another courtyard of the *Mémorial de la Shoah*, I walked through aisles of stone markers that rose like walls, their surfaces smooth except for the more than seventy thousand names incised there. These were France's 75,000 deported Jews. I paused at H and found Hirsch. In 1942, eighty-four Hirsches were deported; in 1943, forty-eight. Berthe and Sigismond were here, Berthe born in 1907, Sigismond in 1906. Their names were rough beneath my touch. Here was something concrete, stone and incision, the mark of a stonecutter's knife as if to say, I am here and you are here.

Inside, I climbed stairs to the third floor, and at the top of the landing I came upon a film playing on a loop. I watched half, then watched it from the beginning. *Les Enfants Avant (The Children Before)*. The film is a series of images without dialogue, scenes of children, boys and girls riding a carousel, a girl sitting with legs crossed on the grass, her fingers holding an imaginary cigarette as she gleefully pretends to smoke. Children visit a zoo and pose with baby lambs; children sit and sing inside a hay wagon. They eat supper with their families. All of this was archival footage from Ukraine and Germany. At the end of the film, a stylized flame erases the children. I thought of Yvonne's recurrent dream — her doll's shattered pieces burning and rising. Always, there is a moment before and a moment after. In between lies what might have been.

10

Another fall when I had returned to France, I made my way to a large square walled by buildings. This was the side of the Marais I knew best, the side where my hotel, Saint Paul le Marais, was located. I followed Rue de Jarente into a large square, its perimeter lined with cafés and outdoor tables under awnings. Always, there were pots with geranium, ivy and impatiens. At Café Saint Catherine, Valerie waited at a corner table. As usual, she was early, and I was a few minutes late. We greeted each other with the customary kisses. "There is a table inside," she said. Remembering our first meeting and an upstairs table, I dutifully followed.

Time after time as Valerie and I rode the Metro to visit with Germaine and Yvonne, then sat in cafés or at dinner afterwards, speaking of what we'd learned, I slowly realized that Valerie, too, had a story to tell. Whenever I asked, she would put me off, saying she did not want to talk about herself or her family. Was she shy? Was she hiding something? I understood these stories were like bruises, tender to the touch. I had hoped our continuing friendship would increase her trust in me, and yes, today, she said, she would speak. "Until the fifties, we had ration tickets," Valerie said. "Clothes came from America, coats, shoes, raincoats. In 1961, I was still dressed in a raincoat given by the Americans. I loved this raincoat. Very military, but good quality." She looked past my shoulder and into the empty restaurant.

"Often, you have asked about my mother," Valerie said. "Now, I will tell you."

During the war, Valerie's mother, a Catholic, was married to a Catholic man. He died of peritonitis in 1943. After the war, her mother married a Jew, and Valerie took on her father's religion and his identity.

"When her first husband died, my mother had a baby, six months old," Valerie said. "Her father-in-law had a house in the country about fifteen kilometers east of Paris. Often, she went there with the baby. This man was a director of a large cosmetics company and received German dignitaries in his home. He was a collaborator. Of course, my mother did not know this. In September of 1944, he flew to Spain."

What she didn't say was that most likely he was escaping reprisal. The summer before, French soldiers, resistance fighters, and the Allies had fought their way to Paris and liberated the city. Soon after, the Allies headed for Germany, and French resistance fighters executed collaborators without trials. Rule of law did not apply.

"The odd thing was," Valerie said, "my mother's father was work-ing with the Resistance. My mother did not know this, either. She was in the countryside when she heard Paris was free. She put her baby in the carriage and set off."

Valerie's mother trudged for miles. She stopped to rest beside the road, lifted her baby from the carriage, offered her breast. Paris was ten miles from her father-in-law's house.

"My mother entered the Bois de Vincennes at dusk. Resistance fighters, German soldiers, and French militiamen were firing. Not all of the city was yet free. My mother kept walking. A truck stopped." Valerie gestured.

She wanted me to name the truck. "An army truck?"

"Yes, yes," she said, quickly. "This man said to her, 'What are you doing here?' She said to him, 'I came back to Paris.' He lifted her up into the truck."

"The baby and the carriage?"

"Yes, yes, everything. So, my mother entered Paris with the army of the liberation. She was twenty years old."

A family legend. A daring young woman walks into danger and winds up riding triumphantly into her city. But there were no cheering crowds, no tricolors waving. Swastikas had not yet been taken down. The streets were full of snipers, bands of resistance fighters, and pockets of German soldiers — all still at war.

Had Valerie's mother suspected her father-in-law's collusion? Was that why she had left his house so quickly? Was she afraid she might be implicated, or was she simply an impulsive twenty-year-old racing for home?

Valerie laced her hands on the table. "When you don't face the truth, the truth comes back to you like a boomerang."

Days later, at the Montparnasse train station, I hurried along a platform. I was leaving Paris and traveling to Valence d'Agen, then on to Auvillar where I was renting a room from Priscilla. My train was two trains, certain cars uncoupling and going in one direction, the rest of the train heading in another. Both my car and my seat were assigned. With my ticket in hand and my terrible French, I asked and found my way to the first train. I wrestled my suitcase up the steps. A conductor was standing nearby, but did not offer a hand. My umbrella, attached to the outside of my suitcase, broke free and tumbled down to the tracks.

Once on the train, I settled into my seat and looked out at cement walls and tracks. On a recent visit, Yvonne told me this story. One day in a café, she and a friend spoke of the war years. This was unusual; her friend wasn't Jewish, and although they'd known eachother for years, neither had mentioned the war to the other. Silence had prevailed. Over coffee, this friend — I'll call her M. — shared a childhood memory. M. and her mother were standing on a platform at this very station, leaving Occupied Paris and traveling to her grandparents' home in the countryside. The child heard screams coming from a sealed box car. She asked her mother, "Why are those people crying?"

"Oh, those people are sick," her mother said. "You must not worry. They will be fine."

Was this M.'s atonement? confession? apology?

⟅⟆

My train slipped from the station, its motion so smooth I barely noticed we were moving until the platform disappeared. We passed through a tunnel and into light. The usual low industrial buildings dominated the landscape. Soon we were south of Paris, passing through villages, then farmland, fields and orchards, vineyards. We were heading for Bordeaux, then on to Agen where I would board a local train and arrive in Valence d'Agen, the closest station to Auvillar.

At Priscilla's River House, my second-floor bedroom was large and sparsely furnished. Thirty years ago, when the Garonne flooded, this house flooded, too, water rising midway to the first-floor windows and spilling into the living room, the kitchen, and halfway up the stairs. When it receded, the water left a damp river smell that oozed through my bedroom walls. I could still smell the musky odor.

I sat at my computer in jeans, a long-sleeved jersey, a sweater, a hat, and fingerless gloves. Priscilla was in Paris. We'd overlapped for a day, met for a visit at the Museum Guimet, and then dinner, but each of us had our own agenda. I was visiting memorial sites, one on the Boulevard de Grenelle, honoring victims who either died or were deported from the Vel d'hiv, the nickname for the infamous cycling stadium Vel D'hiver, now demolished, where French police had housed thousands of Jews — men, women and children — before transporting them to Drancy, the internment camp outside of Paris, then east to their deaths. This memorial was a small, fenced, grassy plot, full of weeds. A crumpled piece of paper rested beside a clump of dandelions. Silently, I recited the first five words of the Kaddish, the Jewish prayer for the dead, because those were the only words I knew.

Now, I was alone in Priscilla's house following her rules. In Paris, she'd been clear. If I turned on the heat, she'd charge me more. How much more, she didn't know. She'd agreed to share her bicycle, but then said I'd need to buy her a new lock and chain. I didn't want to argue about money. I hated to argue about money. I also disliked ambiguity. I closed my computer and looked out the window at the red-tiled roof of the house next door. I remembered our walk on the *Chemin*. Even then, I'd felt used. Priscilla had asked me to secure our ride. She'd sent me to the pharmacy to buy sunscreen and bug repellent, both expensive items. Now, I was cold, but I didn't turn on the heat.

I told myself that in spite of my discomfort, I was pleased to be back in my beloved village of Auvillar and falling again into its rhythm. I was at ease flying alone across the sea, touring Paris, riding the Metro, and settling into life in this village. I loved hanging my wash outside on a line, climbing the hill to the *centre-ville* and picking figs along the way. Perhaps, my friendship with Priscilla wasn't as mutual as I would like. Perhaps, I was being petty. With the new lock and chain in the front basket, I wheeled the bicycle from the garage. I was en route to the Peugeot dealer's, the only nearby source of a rental car. With Germaine and Valerie's help, I'd planned a trip to Beaulieu sur Dordogne, where Monsieur Le Hech, a local historian and friend of Germaine's, would speak with me and show me *la colonie*. I couldn't believe I'd come this far with my miserable French — a planned visit to *la colonie*, a place of mystery and awe. Priscilla had agreed to navigate and translate.

Riding Priscilla's bicycle, I followed a roundabout and chose a safer, less traveled route to Valence d'Agen, passing fields of sorghum and sunflowers gone to seed. The road was narrow and flanked by ditches. No shoulder. Still, a driver sped past, leaving me little space. I held tight to the handlebars and stiffened my resolve. *Keep the wheel steady. Do not swerve.* The back of the car disappeared. I was alone, sitting up high on this old-fashioned bike, passing peach and apple orchards, the apple crop heavy and ready for picking. I remembered our walk on the *Chemin*, Priscilla telling me about France's fertile soil, a nearly perfect PH. That was what had made France strong, Priscilla had said. France fed her laborers as they built the grand châteaux along the Loire. She fed her soldiers as they fought her wars. In France, food was not only sustenance, it was abundance and beauty. Those laborers and soldiers had eaten well.

I crossed a bridge and climbed a short hill into the center of Valence d'Agen. I passed the fountains with colored water, passed the railroad station, and followed a road I'd never taken.

At the Peugeot dealer's, I leaned Priscilla's bicycle against the side of the showroom window. No way to lock it. Priscilla would not have approved. At a high counter, I waited patiently for my turn. Only one man behind the counter. I quickly discerned he was the owner. "Yes, yes," he said to me, "I have two cars that I rent. Both are *normal*." He pronounced the word the French way, accent on the second syllable.

"*Nor-mal?*"

He made shifting motions with his hand.

The last time I had driven a stick-shift was my red Datsun in the '70s. Before that I had an MG, also red, a sporty car Dick and I bought shortly after our marriage, that I drove while pregnant with my first son. By the end of my pregnancy, I couldn't fit my belly under the steering wheel. Dick drove me to the hospital and when I left, my newborn in my arms, Dick was at the wheel of our brand new black Ford Falcon station wagon, and that, I joked, was the metaphor for my life, MG to Ford, sporty car to station wagon.

The summer after my sophomore year in college, I drove a Hillman Minx with a column-mounted gear shift, and although I had paid for the car with money I'd earned, my father was the one who found it and negotiated the deal for me. I'd never heard of a Hillman Minx. No one had. And for good reason. The thing kept throwing fan belts. Late at night driving home from the Jersey Shore, I'd break down and telephone from an all-night gas station, "Dad, I'm stuck again."

Surprisingly, he didn't yell, simply said, "Do what you have to do."

❧

The Peugeot dealer waited for my answer. He was a man in his mid-forties, tall and broad with wavy dark hair, younger than any of my three sons. "*Oui*," I said. "No *problème*."

Leaving his parking lot and Priscilla's bicycle, which he assured me would be fine, we went for a test run. I gripped the steering wheel of the black Peugeot with two fists. A stream of oncoming traffic flowed past. I eased in, riding the clutch, and immediately approached a roundabout. I shifted. The car stuttered, then settled into second. Now third. I was okay on a straight stretch. I downshifted, rode the clutch, turned right. Another straight stretch in third. I never did get to fourth before I was back in the dealer's lot, turning the key and thinking: *There is no way this man will rent me this car*. I dropped the key into his palm. His face was kind. "You will learn. It won't take long."

❧

At the house, Priscilla stood at the counter beside the sink and sliced a tomato. She'd arrived late the night before without notice. I dropped my backpack onto a kitchen chair. After finding a space heater in a closet, I'd carried it downstairs. If I couldn't turn on central heat, I'd have warmth in the kitchen. We'd agreed to split the electric bill. I switched on the heater and sat with my back to the coils. Priscilla turned. "Now he wants me to accompany him to South America. I don't think I want to go."

The man she lived with — sometimes. Not the man in Boston, the Charlottesville man, the man who traveled for work and at this moment was still in Paris. This was the man for whom she'd designed the garden where birds fed, rabbits foraged, and a snake sunned, oblivious to one another.

I poured myself a glass of wine and returned to my seat in front of the heater. "Why don't you want to go to South America?"

"Ah, cherie, it's complicated. Maybe later."

I sipped the local red, then paused, holding the glass mid-air. "Well, I did it. I reserved the car."

"Ah, cherie, I'm afraid I can't go with you after all. I must stay at home this weekend."

I set my glass on the table. "Priscilla, we've had this trip planned for weeks."

"You see, I thought we would go through Bordeaux."

"I told you Bordeaux was nowhere near Beaulieu sur Dordogne."

"Ah, cherie, I should have checked a map sooner. You see, I have business in Bordeaux."

Now, I was the one who needed her. I didn't know the roads. I couldn't drive and read a map at the same time. My French was lousy. I was bad at *nor-mal*. Still, I had to do this. "So, Monsieur Le Hech speaks English?" Priscilla said.

"Why do you ask?"

"I'm wondering how you will manage."

Without answering, I stood and shouldered my backpack.

"Going out?" she asked.

"For a bit."

At Moulin à Nef, John and I pored over a map. He charted my route. I would stick to country roads and avoid the AutoRoute. Prettier and less stressful. According to Valerie, Monsieur Le Hech spoke a little English, but she would email my questions to him in French, just in case.

John folded the map and handed it back. "You'll be fine," he said. "People do this all the time. Trust me. You'll make it."

At the River House, the kitchen was empty. I prepared my supper, an omelet with *cèpes* — small brown flavorful mushrooms — fresh green beans and hunks of baguette. I sipped the wine I'd left earlier. Priscilla entered the kitchen and eyed my plate. "I thought perhaps you'd gone out for supper."

I shook my head, refilled my glass. Priscilla poured from my bottle. "If you don't mind. I'll pay you back." She leaned her back against the counter. "I suppose I should have told you sooner."

I slid a slice of my omelet onto my fork. "I'm all set."

"But you're not going?"

"Of course, I'm going."

"Cherie, how can you with your French?"

My eyebrows pinched. "Actually," I said, drawing the syllables long, "I'm looking forward to the challenge."

11

The rise of the blue metal suspension bridge disappeared into dense fog. In Valence d'Agen, I passed through ghostly streets and neighborhoods I'd never seen on market days. According to MapQuest, Beaulieu sur Dordogne was two hours and twelve minutes away along the country roads John had chosen for me. I left at nine for an appointment at two. I thought of Priscilla. *Ah, cherie, how will you manage with your French?* I wrestled the car into third, then fourth, and gave it gas. *I can do this. I will do this.*

Trucks emerged from the fog and sped toward me. I slowed. A car passed on my left and I glimpsed a disgusted look on the driver's face. I was driving too slowly, especially for the French. My folded map sat on the passenger's seat, my route highlighted in orange. I tried to read my handwritten directions and drive at the same time, looking down, looking up. At roundabouts, all top arrows pointed to Paris. I was not driving to Paris. I was driving to Beaulieu sur Dordogne. Below Paris, each arrow pointed to places I didn't know. I circled each roundabout once, twice, looking for a village that sounded familiar, a name I'd seen on my map. Anxious about where I was going, I exited, drove for maybe twenty minutes and had a funny feeling. I pulled over and checked my map. A river on my right should have been on my left. I turned around. Same rotary. Different exit.

The landscape changed. I passed through an industrial town with flat-roofed buildings and loading docks. The road narrowed on the outskirts, and suddenly sun broke through fog and clouds. A sign pointed up a hill: Montoc. I'd never heard of Montoc. Still, I checked my rearview mirror before hitting the lever of my turn signal and veering right. A steep winding road led me to a charming hilltop village. A few stores. A restaurant. A bar with a stone terrace where people sat reading newspapers, chatting, and drinking coffee. I angled the car into a parking space. This was not like me. I didn't usually change course. I sat back and looked through the windshield at hills and fields and let time settle slowly on my skin.

On the terrace, I centered my chair into a circle of sun and waited for my double espresso. Geraniums bloomed in clay pots, and vinca vine trailed purple flowers. Around me, the sounds of French and English — a village of British ex-pats. I eavesdropped on conversations about birthdays, lunches, and plans for a light supper. I lingered in warmth and familiarity. I didn't want to leave.

Back on the road, I figured out two things about roundabouts: one, the farthest destination was written in the largest letters at the top of each sign, thus the arrows pointing to Paris; and two, by the time I looked down the long list, I couldn't sort through all the names. I needed to disregard Paris and circle each roundabout three times to find a village with a name I'd seen on my map. In this way, Beaulieu sur Dordogne eventually made its way onto a sign post.

I entered the village crossing a bridge and there, on the other side of a main square, I saw my hotel, *Le Manoir de Beaulieu*, a large building that looked far seedier than its photograph on the internet. It was seedy inside, too, a gloomy lobby furnished with low-slung dusky pink couches and stiff-backed wooden chairs, seats upholstered with worn burgundy fabric. At the back of the lobby, a man sat at a compact bar drinking a beer. I saw no one else. The reception was nothing more than a closet with a half door and a shelf. I wanted to flee. Instead, I took the key a clerk offered.

Thankfully, my room was clean and neat with stark white bedding. The bathroom had been modernized and it, too, was clean, with big fluffy white towels. Most important, I was here in Beaulieu sur Dordogne, the village that had saved seventy Jewish refugee girls living in *la colonie*, saved Germaine and her children, Yvonne and her family, and approximately two hundred others.

When Germaine asked if I'd like to visit *la colonie*, I didn't hesitate. "Oh, yes," I said, knowing instinctively a visit would deepen my understanding of Vichy France. Then, once again, I doubted myself. Who was I to keep chasing down this story? And how would I get there? Her days in Beaulieu sur Dordogne, Germaine said at our first meeting, were the happiest days of her life. It was as if she wanted me to see those days, touch those days and feel them.

❧

I wandered down a narrow, cobbled street to the river, passing a large church on my right, a square on my left. The village was not as small as Auvillar, but small enough. I would not get lost. I stopped for lunch on the terrace of a nicer hotel and sipped from a glass of chilled white wine, feeling decadent. At home I did not drink wine with lunch. A waiter brought my salad with grilled shrimp. I tore hunks from a baguette. I savored my food. At a little before two, I entered the *Office de Tourisme*, my assigned meeting place. A man stepped out from behind a tall counter. "Sandell?"

"Monsieur Le Hech?"

Monsieur Le Hech had a square face and dark eyes. He wore

half-framed glasses and reeked of cigarettes. At a table, he spoke fondly of Germaine, particularly of her visit here in 2006 when the village had held an event to commemorate *la colonie* and remember the children and their caretakers, and to remember, too, those villagers who had helped. With his minimal English, my bumbling French, Valerie's translations, and our gestures, we not only managed, we enjoyed one another's company. Together, we looked at photographs in the *History of Beaulieu Sur Dordogne*, the book Germaine had shown me, a book I bought that day. Monsieur Le Hech stood. "Would you like to see?"

"Oh, yes." I said.

Outside the *Office de Tourisme*, Monsieur Le Hech lit up a Gauloise. I, an ex-smoker, remembered that first drag when I would pull the smoke down into my lungs. Nearly forty years had passed since my last cigarette; yet, at this moment, I wanted the pleasure of that first drag. I wondered what had brought about this sudden urge for a smoke. But I would not ask Monsieur Le Hech for a cigarette. Instead, I walked and inhaled the second-hand smoke.

This was the street I'd followed earlier and this was the church I'd passed, the massive Abbey of Saint Peter with its heavy, dark, wooden doors and its clock tower. I'd breezed past without noticing the bronze statue of the Virgin and Child. Now, I lingered and read the street sign, *Place de la Bridolle.*

The day had turned summer hot. Despite the heat, Monsieur Le Hech had dressed as most Frenchmen do, in dark colors, with black trousers, gray wool sweater, and a short black leather jacket he wore unzipped. I too wore black — black skirt, black cap-sleeved silk top, and a short black cardigan that I slipped from my shoulders and tied at my waist. Even my sandals were black.

Monsieur Le Hech gestured to a cocoa-brown stucco building with shuttered windows. Ivy climbed the walls. "*La Colonie.*"

Here? In the heart of the village? Next to the abbey? So much for my fantasy of a country farmhouse. I stepped closer. The thick-growing ivy nearly covered a plaque. I lifted leaves and translated:

Here from 1939 to 1944 in Beaulieu sur Dordogne refugee children and children from the Occupied Zone were saved from deportation and murder in this colony organized by the Jewish Scouts of France and directed by Monsieur and Madame Gordin. Thanks to the help and dedication of many in Beaulieu including Adrienne Laquièze. Righteous Among the Nations.

The past lay close to this building and close to the earth on which it stood, and they were here, touching the air, touching my skin — Madame Gordin, Germaine, Yvonne, and the unknown girls living inside *la colonie*. Adrienne Laquièze, a Catholic woman in her mid-twenties, was here, too. Her parents had run a restaurant directly across the plaza and lived in rooms above. Monsieur and Madame Laquièze also owned *la colonie*, and they knowingly and willingly rented to the Jewish Scouts. In their flat above the restaurant, Monsieur and Madame Laquièze sheltered the youngest of the Jewish children, leaving them in Adrienne's care. What I knew of Adrienne and her family, I'd learned from Germaine.

One day back in 1943, when Adrienne held a Jewish child in her arms, an officer of the Milice, the dreaded Vichy paramilitary organization that tortured, murdered, and hunted resistance workers and Jews, entered the restaurant. Generally, arrests were not arbitrary; they came with orders. However, that night the Milice officer told Adrienne to hand over the child. In a photograph in the *History of Beaulieu Sur Dordogne*, Adrienne is pictured in profile, her dark hair swept back from her face, her long slim nose her dominant feature. Smiling, she looked approachable and kind. She whispered in the child's ear and spoke the words Germaine had repeated to me, "Cry, loudly. Tell him you have a stomach ache." Adriènne turned from the crying child and eyed the Milice officer. "The child is ill. She needs a hospital. I must leave."

The officer stepped aside.

Strange as this may seem considering the cruelty of the Milice, certain officers, Germaine said, treated the sick with respect. Perhaps this was the reason, perhaps not. Times were odd and complex. Maybe the officer harbored a certain feeling for Adriènne or saw something in that Jewish child that reminded him of his own child. Possibly he was tired, worn out, worn down, and he didn't know why he'd asked in the first place. Perhaps all he'd really wanted was a drink at the bar.

This was the plaza where the girls had held hands and formed a six-pointed Star of David. This was where they'd sung *Ma Tovu*, a Hebrew melody that Germaine had passed off as "oriental." In the photograph in *History of Beaulieu Sur Dordogne*, Germaine stood at one of the points of the six-pointed-star, arms raised and ready to give the downbeat. I imagined Yvonne standing off to one side, her whole body yearning to sing.

Monsieur Le Hech pointed upward. "You see?"

Red roof tiles. Blue sky. A balcony. Ah, an inner courtyard. In *History of Beaulieu Sur Dordogne*, there is a photograph of girls scrubbing blouses on washboards, of girls twisting and wringing clothes by hand, all lifting their eyes to the photographer. Above their heads the posts of this same balcony. Someone was documenting daily life here, and now I understood the necessity of performing everyday tasks to keep the monsters of doubt and fear at a distance. I wondered what the girls had known of one another, what they'd sensed of this village and of the war. How doubt, dread and trepidation must have burrowed through skin and into bone.

I wanted to go inside *la colonie*, but the British couple who owned this house had left for the winter, shuttering the place until spring. The interior must have changed considerably since Germaine shared a room with Paulette, *nom de guerre* Sultan, her best friend. In one of Germaine's photographs, both girls sat on a bed, Sultan smiling, happy and young, Germaine remote, as if her thoughts were elsewhere. She seemed older than Sultan and less carefree. Germaine wore a coat; Sultan did not. I wondered if moments before that photo, Germaine had returned from a rendezvous with Ralph. I wondered if they'd already married. I wondered if Germaine was announcing to Sultan that she was pregnant.

Prominent in the photograph a large radio sat atop a bedside table. Wires looped, following an outside wall along a window. An antenna. Secretly, at night, Germaine and Sultan listened to French Free Radio, Madame Gordin stage-whispering, "Girls, turn the volume down."

All of this had happened here, in this place. It was not impossible; you *could* reach back and touch the past.

That evening, as I stepped inside *Le Velouté*, the restaurant once owned by the *Laquièze* family, a quick glance told me I was the only diner. I liked the ambiance of others when I dined alone, and in another circumstance, I might have turned and left, but this was where I wanted to be, sitting at a window table inside *Le Velouté* and looking out at the lighted *Place de la Bridolle* and the ivy-covered stucco walls of *la colonie*. I ordered the *églegin* — a fish of some kind — and a glass of the house red. Sitting back, I looked out the window and thought of Germaine and Sultan inside *la colonie*, two young women sitting side by side on a single bed.

Sultan's story did not turn out so well. Her first husband, a soldier, died in the war. Her second husband died of cancer. Her third husband died of old age. Sultan had three children. "Poor Sultan," Germaine had said. "Her first child was mentally slow; her second became a

127

gangster; her third won a Nobel Prize, but he is not very nice. He does not visit his mother. Sultan used to manage. Now, she does not manage. She lives in a home for old people."

～

On the other side of the *Place de la Bridolle*, the white wooden door of *la colonie* shone beneath a street lamp. Was that the door? Or was it the door around the corner on *rue de la République*? Did he come in the day or in the night, Amédée Duhaut, the friendly gendarme who warned of roundups? No German soldiers bivouacked in this village. They were in Brive, coming only when they were off duty to stroll the quiet streets, or on duty to make arrests. Before a roundup, they sent their paperwork on ahead, and French police made the arrests. Why did Duhaut take on this task? He was not from this village, Monsieur Le Hech had told me earlier. He had no relatives here. This was his wartime posting. After the war, he left as inconspicuously as he'd arrived. Yet, on days when he saw those orders, Duhaut slipped away from the gendarmerie and walked the quiet streets of Beaulieu sur Dordogne to *la colonie*. He knocked. Sitting at this window, I pictured him, a man of average height, wearing a blue uniform, his badge glinting, his step slow and steady. Madame Gordin answered the door. "You must go away," Duhaut said. "The Germans will come."

In those days of German occupation, anti-Semitic propaganda filled the airwaves, and in newspapers cartoons depicted Jews as short, bulbous men with claw-like fingers, thick lips, and droopy ears. Printed flyers featured French priests dressed in their robes and collars calling Jews Christ-killers. Yet here in Beaulieu sur Dordogne, Jewish children and their caretakers lived among the villagers. "*Tout le monde* knew this was a Jewish house," Monsieur Le Hech had said. Everyone knew.

I thought of Germaine riding her bicycle to Brive and bringing meat to Josette, her sister. The butcher liked her, she'd said to me, and he gave her extra meat. On a road between Beaulieu sur Dordogne and Brive, a gendarme asked for her papers. He read her last name, Rousso, an Italian name. He accused Germaine of being a spy and arrested her. Madame Gordin arrived at the gendarmerie. "She is a *chieftain* with the Scouts," Madame said. "She takes care of children." Germaine went free. The only time police had arrested her, she had been mistaken for an Italian spy — not a Jew.

I imagined the villagers walking to prayer all those years ago. A priest would have been standing outside the opened, massive door of the Abbey of Saint Peter, welcoming his parishioners with *la colonie* in plain view. Had this priest preached a Catholicism similar to the type Archbishop Jules Gerard Saliège preached in Toulouse? Saliège had read a pastoral letter to all Catholics, proclaiming: "The Jews are men; the Jewesses are women. The foreigners are men and women. One may not do anything one wishes to these men, to these women, to these fathers and mothers. They are part of the human race; they are our brothers, like so many others. A Christian cannot forget this."

I thought of my meeting with Monsieur Le Hech, the two of us strolling to the river. "Some people," he said, "were very sympathetic. Some not very much. Most people in France during the war were aware only of finding food. They didn't resist; they didn't cooperate. They waited for the war to stop."

Inside *Le Velouté*, history breathed through these walls. Stories of Monsieur Duhaut, Madame Gordin, Monsieur and Madame Laquièze, Adriènne and Germaine. All of them must have come to this restaurant for a glass of wine, a smile, and a laugh. The place would have looked different then, no newly refinished floorboards with their shellacked blond mirror-like surface, no freshly oiled dark beams, no stark-white painted ceiling, no lime-green walls with a single wall painted violet red. What had possessed the owners to paint such garish colors?

Chances were that, back when Germaine was here, these walls would have been dingy, the floorboards dusty and marked with footprints. I pressed the soles of my sandals and made an imprint over imprints. If Germaine's footprints were here, so too were those of the village doctor who had treated the children when they were ill, and of Zozo — not his real name — who had owned a hardware store and fixed what needed fixing inside *la colonie*, a faucet, a broken pipe, a stopped-up sink. If their imprints were here, so too were those of the Milice officer who on that evening chose to let a child live.

Ordinary life. Daily life. Extraordinary decisions that meant survival.

My dinner arrived. The fish looked and tasted like haddock and arrived on a bed of buttery braised cabbage and leeks. My waiter spoke English with a Scottish accent. He was one of the owners. He did the serving; his partner cooked. As he refilled my water glass, I asked if he knew the history of this building. He knew of another restaurant before this one. "And before that?"

He stepped back. "A hotel."

I lifted my glass to the ghosts that lingered.

When *la colonie* closed, the Jewish Scouts made plans to move the children.

In my fantasy it was night. A black sedan with rounded fenders and a long hood idled outside *la colonie*, Adrienne Laquièze in the driver's seat. She tapped ash from a cigarette and tucked a strand of hair into her upswept twist. She checked her rearview mirror and glanced toward *la colonie*. A door opened. Girls hurried out. They crowded into the backseat. Some sat on the floor. Germaine gave them kisses and wished them all a safe journey. Yvonne was not among them. She had left with Claude, a cousin who worked with the resistance.

Adriènne motored slowly, but not too slowly. She must not call attention to herself or to the car. If arrested, she would face the same fate as the children — deportation, maybe torture, certain death.

~

Sipping from a second glass of the house merlot, I wondered what France would look like today if every village had had a population like that of Beaulieu sur Dordogne, a gendarme like Monsieur Duhaut, a family like the Laquièze family. Monsieur Le Hech's words played in my head. "*Toute le monde* knew it was a Jewish house."

Was I impossibly naïve to think we can learn to put humanity first and stand together, even silently? Not on a large scale; that is impossible. But individually. For that, it seemed, was what had saved the Jews sheltering in Beaulieu sur Dordogne, a certain quiet, collective, yet independent understanding. And a desire, not particularly to do good, but at least to do no harm. One hundred or so adult Jews sheltering in this region survived. Of the seventy girls sheltering in *la colonie*, all were saved except one, the child so lonely she returned home to her family in Paris, all murdered in the camps.

Adrienne died in 1998. A year later, the Israeli government honored her posthumously as Righteous Among the Nations, Germaine nominating her for the medal. At a ceremony in Paris, Germaine spoke. Here is Valerie's translation. "Very dear Adrienne, who more than you deserves the Medal of the Righteous? ... Arbiter, protector, one who hides and conveys Jewish children to Switzerland, especially dangerous, exposing yourself to death by shooting or to arrest and a concentration camp. You did this and you wanted nothing in return for what you thought was your duty."

Adrienne's son, Claude Guichard, accepted the medal on his mother's behalf.

On my last evening in Beaulieu, I walked to the *Place de la Bridolle*,

Germaine's story, Sultan's story, the girls' stories, all spiraling inside of me. The night was mild, the sky full of stars. Streetlamps lighted my way. Alone in the plaza, I touched a leaf. English ivy was sacred to Dionysus, the Greek god of wine, fertility, ecstasy, and the theater. The plant grew densely, its aerial root-like structures holding fast to the stucco façade of *la colonie*.

Again, I imagined Adrienne Laquièze at the wheel of that black sedan. I had no idea how this escape actually happened, but they did escape. They lived.

I ran the pads of my fingers over the raised letters of the plaque. I would probably not visit this place again, and I wanted to carry memory in my touch.

In the lobby of my hotel, a man sat at the compact bar, shoulders hunched. Over his head, a French drama played on a flat-screen television. He eyed me in that way of men. Too old for an appraising stare, I ignored his curiosity and took my key from the clerk's hand. As always, the stairway was dark. I held the banister and felt my way, touching each riser with the toe of my sandal. In an upstairs corridor, I waved my arms, tripped a motion sensor, and walked quickly to my door before the light clicked off.

Sleepless in my bed, I listened to bells in the abbey ring the hour, their sound reverberating through these walls. I fell backwards into time, Germaine's time in this village, my time when I was a child lying awake in my bed inside my yellow stucco house. Our time overlapped, Germaine's early adulthood and my early childhood.

The French philosopher Gaston Bachelard wrote of our houses, saying, "If I were asked to name the chief benefit of the house, I should say: the house shelters day-dreaming, the house protects the dreamer, the house allows one to dream in peace." In places far and near, Germaine, Yvonne and I dreamed of shelter and peace. We dreamed our futures.

132

Before leaving Beaulieu sur Dordogne, I drove into the countryside. The macadam was narrow, and when an occasional car passed I downshifted and pulled to my right. The Peugeot dealer was correct, I had learned to drive this car.

12

One day in Auvillar, walking up the steep hill into the *centre-ville*, I stumbled across a poster propped inside the window of an empty house. In the upper left, a red J, and under it overlapping photographs of a man, a woman, and a girl. The girl was maybe sixteen or seventeen, probably the couple's daughter. These were Vichy identity photos, the red J indicating these people were Jews.

The girl held my interest. She was on the cusp — no longer a child and not yet a woman. Although not classically beautiful or glamorous, she had an allure. In the photo, her long dark hair is pulled back from her face and fastened with barrettes, a style that is no longer fashionable. She pouts and stares, her gaze defiant, perhaps knowing.

The poster was a collage of images — a postage stamp with a photo of Marshall Pétain, an eagle with talons holding a swastika, a photo of a large crowd, all the images in black and white except for the red J and the red of these words: *Des rafles à la déportation, Auvillar. Société Auvillaraise Culturelle Franco-Allemande.*

Rafles à la déportation were roundups. The French and German Cultural Society was the organization Gerhard and Mary Jo, his wife, had founded. This was a commemoration. Of what? A roundup of Jews? Here? Was I translating correctly? I thought I knew Auvillar's Jewish history, the Hirsch family fleeing Occupied Paris, Sigismond's and Berthe's arrest by the Gestapo; their son, Jean, finding refuge with the Ursuline nuns and then moving on to Provence and the protection of Doctor Daniel. I knew of no other Jews in Auvillar. Of no deportations. Why hadn't Gerhard told me about this?

Without alerting him of my visit, I knocked on his door. Graciously, he invited me in and poured coffee. He pulled a larger version of the poster from beneath a stack of papers. "I tried to tell you," he said. "You only wanted to hear about Hirsch."

This was true. I'd been searching for a single story. Now, I was opening to other voices, collecting bits and pieces and hoping that later, I would figure out how to make sense of what I was learning. What was also true was that Gerhard rambled, and often, I'd wanted to lead him back to my question. My need to focus was both an asset and a flaw. Today, I would have to listen.

Gerhard spoke of a day, maybe ten years ago, when he was searching German sites on the internet. "I had no purpose. I found mention of Auvillar. Well, Auvillar is such a small place..." He paused. "I was surprised." He learned of a symposium in Graz, Austria, where panelists spoke of a discovery inside the *mairie* in Auvillar. "Imagine," Gerhard said.

I pictured a workman unlocking an attic door and seeing a number of old leather suitcases, all covered with nearly five decades of dust and fallen plaster, all officially sealed with yellow tape, labeled, and dated by the gendarmerie: *August 26, 1942*. The workman knew what he had found and quickly alerted authorities. Only a government official could break those seals. "Can you believe it, from Auvillar to Graz and back to Auvillar?" Gerhard said.

"No one here told you?" I asked.

"No one. I found this out myself." I looked down at the poster Gerhard had set at my place. "It is too bad you were not here for the commemoration. We had many people, not just from Auvillar. They came from all over. This was a wonderful girl. Wonderful." The girl in the poster. "She was called Adèle."

"Deported?" I said.

"Deported."

"From Auvillar?"

"Yes, from Auvillar."

Adèle was the seventeen-year-old daughter of Bruno and Gisèle Kurzweil, all pictured on Gerhard's poster. After the war no one claimed their possessions, so their suitcases, all packed for travel, languished until Pascal Caïla, an historian, broke the seals. Roger Téchiné, a representative from the mayor's office, and two members of the Jewish community from Montauban were there. Caïla, also from Montauban, set up a video camera. "It is possible for you to see this on YouTube," Gerhard said.

Later, I did, watching as Pascal Caïla reverently unpacked each suitcase, lifting photographs — a picture of Adèle posing jauntily with a friend, another of Adèle standing behind a seated woman, perhaps her aunt. I saw a resemblance. There was a photograph of the family vacationing at a seaside resort. There were Adèle's dresses, her books, her bottle of eau de cologne, her diploma from the Lycée Jules Michelet in Montauban, her phonograph, her watercolors. Adèle loved to draw and paint. In the video, Caïla lifted her drawings. He lifted Gisèle's blouses and black suede shoes stuffed with newspaper to keep their shape. Bruno's umbrella, his books, his two spare pairs of glasses, one gray and one tortoise shell. He unpacked the family's cutlery, an entire set.

⋘

In March of 1938, the Kurzweil family had fled Graz and arrived in

Paris. At Montmorency, a school for Jewish refugee children on the outskirts of the city, Adèle met Hanna Papanek, also from Graz. The girls became friends. In June 1940, as the German Army advanced, the girls and their families fled a second time — Hanna and her parents to the States, the Kurzweils to Montauban, a city about an hour's train ride from Auvillar.

In Graz, Bruno Kurzweil had been a lawyer. In Paris and in Montauban, he worked with the Jewish resistance, securing false identity papers for refugee Jews. Ironically, while others left, he waited for his own papers, visas from the Mexican Consulate that were late. In June 1942, Jewish officials in Montauban moved the Kurzweils and three other families to Auvillar. Safe housing was tight in Montauban. Everyday life, that's what these people wanted, a place to set a table for dinner, to read a book, to listen to music.

Caïla spent a month taking inventory of the family's possessions; yet, few in this village knew of the suitcases or these families. Perhaps, they chose not to know. As I had discovered, even today, Auvillar continues to bury its wartime history in France's deep silence. Villagers wanted to forget Vichy. All the French wanted to forget Vichy. Somehow word of the discovery in Auvillar traveled to the Austrian Cultural Forum in New York City, and the Forum announced the finding in a newsletter. Perhaps Caïla was the source. Then, reading that newsletter in the States, Hanna Papanek recognized a photograph of Adèle, her old school friend.

Gerhard lifted his hand to the back of his neck. He'd read the Forum's newsletter on the internet. "Before that moment, I knew nothing of those families. Nobody knew. Memory changes."

Perhaps, he means memory shifts. Or disappears.

"I know this from Germany. If, in a certain house, deportations took place, there is no memory," Gerhard said. Light shone through a squat window high on one wall, casting Gerhard's face in shadow.

I remembered a story my youngest son told of visiting a Jewish cemetery in Germany with an old man who remembered the war. Knowing my son was Jewish, the man apologized. "I am sorry. We did not know."

"Bullshit," I said to my son when he told me this story. That was how angry I was at this familiar German refrain: We did not know.

My son believed his friend, the old man. I believed that by taking my son to that cemetery and showing him the well-tended graves, the man wished to atone — to a Jew. Yes, he was sorry, so why not acknowledge that on some level everyone knew? Perhaps not the details of the camps and the murders, but of the slow erosion of each and every Jew's autonomy and eventual disappearance?

In *Not I*, Joachim Fest's memoir about his father Johannes Fest — a cultural conservative, fierce supporter of the Weimar Republic, and an opponent of Hitler — he gives the reader a front-row seat as events of the Third Reich unfold. Johannes loses his job; his friends withdraw; he receives anonymous calls warning of a Gestapo visit. A German and a Christian, he is alarmed and agitated at the suffering of his Jewish friends and their eventual disappearance. *Not I* — the German title is *Just Say Nein* — shows National Socialism permeating every aspect of German life: grammar schools, high schools, universities, parks, playgrounds, stores, doctors' offices, and neighborhoods. There were few Germans like Johannes Fest who asked about their Jewish neighbors: Where did they go? Why haven't we heard? On some level, everyone knew.

In post-war France, it was not National Socialism and the Nazis that were taboo; it was Collaboration. The Vichy government not only carried out Nazi orders of deportation, but initiated their own, most infamously the deportations of children when French police deported the parents and then, not knowing what to do with all those Jewish orphans, loaded teens, ten-year-olds, five-year-olds, and toddlers into cattle cars bound for the east. René Bousquet, secretary general of the Vichy police, directed those operations in Paris.

Gerhard refilled my cup. "The French," he said, "are not at the point we had been in forty-five, forty-six, forty-seven, forty-eight. All of this clearing of the past."

He was telling me the French had been slow to confront this history, and they continued to be slow.

At Gerhard's event, *Journée Histoire et Mémoire*, Pascal Caïla spoke, and a filmmaker showed a film about the roundups of 1942. Gerhard had wanted plaques attached to buildings where each of the four families had lived. "I knew there were addresses for these families, but when I went to the *mairie*, no one could find the papers. This was not unusual. Often papers from those years disappeared. I started asking old people. Do you know something? Do you remember? No one knew. Then, one day, an old woman takes me aside. She says to me, 'She used to come into my mother's shop. She had beautiful hair.'"

Adèle.

Gerhard said to me, "You pass this place where she lived every day. It is the soap shop. They lived in rooms above."

My friend lowered his chin and hunched his broad shoulders. "This period is very difficult to understand. The Vichy regime was based on anti-Communism, and Europe was afraid of becoming Communist. Already, Spain had nearly become Communist. Catholic people had been on the side of Vichy."

At first, I didn't understand — *Catholic people on the side of Vichy.* That didn't seem possible or probable. Then I realized that Fascism was the lesser of two evils. When faced with Godless Communism versus Fascism, many Catholics chose Fascism. Besides, the Church had a long history of anti-Semitism, blaming Jews for Christ's death and coming up with the blood libel, a mistaken Medieval belief that Jews needed the blood of a Christian child to make matzo at Passover, a myth that still cropped up in anti-Semitic rants and anti-Semitic literature. Jews believed in the sanctity of human life. Blood sacrifice was forbidden. Wasn't that the point of the Abraham and Isaac story?

Gerhard said, "Now, French people are criticizing Vichy. I am more clement. I think we don't have to judge these people. The German force was very strong. Maybe it was better to cooperate in this way."

My belly contracted. *Criticizing Vichy. Better to cooperate?* I mulled his words. It wasn't until 1995 that President Jacques Chirac publicly recognized France's responsibility for deporting Jews during the *Shoah*. For years, the French had wanted to shift blame back to Vichy, exonerating the French State. Some still do.

"Nobody knows exactly these things, and much *refoulement*..."

"*Refoulement?*"

He switched from French to German. "*Verdrabgen.*"

I didn't know either word. Gerhard explained. "Freud invented this name, *refoule*. It is an unconscious act."

"Ah, repression."

"Yes. Memory doesn't accept the things that are negative. Many things about the Jewish accident..."

Accident? Did he just say accident? I stared at the wall of ancient narrow bricks and made excuses for my friend. He was groping for a word. Maybe having a problem with translation. English was his third language, French his second, German his first. I thought of the words *Shoah* and Holocaust. In modern Hebrew, *Shoah* translates as catastrophe, a word that reverberated. Holocaust meant burning and brought to mind total annihilation, something finished or done, not damage that leaked up through time into an ever-continuing present.

Gerhard was a good man, a kind man, and as I ran his monologue through my head I wondered what my muteness said about me. Was I a coward? An opportunist? A bystander? I didn't know. But the word stayed with me: *accident.*

Understanding crept into Gerhard's eyes. He'd chosen the wrong word. He stood and paced. "Many things about the *Shoah* in Europe are *verdrabgen.*"

Repressed.

"Anti-Semitism in Europe is an old story, eh?" Gerhard said.

Neither of us had grown up without bias. I had inherited my parents' and my grandparents' prejudices against Germany and Germans, my father mocking a German accent, me as a child goose-stepping and imitating the stereotype of a German soldier. Post-war my father would not buy a German car. His pride in his German Jewish heritage took a back seat to his feelings about the Nazis. Not that he talked about his feelings. The subject of the *Shoah* was taboo. Shameful. How could those Jews — not us, but them — have allowed themselves to be led like sheep to the slaughter? I inhaled the scent of my father's biases, his stereotypes, his callousness.

When my husband Dick and I were in middle-age and he had business in Austria, we traveled to both Austria and Germany. We met and spoke with Germans, all of us congenial, but under my pleasant façade I was uneasy. I bristled at their accents. I wondered about their families. Where had they been in 1933, 1938, or 1942? What had they seen? What had they known? One night, as we were passing a bar, a group of drunk young men stumbled onto the sidewalk singing *Ein Prosit,* a German drinking song, and its martial beat sent chills along the length of my spine. I gripped Dick's hand. On that cobbled narrow street with its ancient buildings rising from a sidewalk, I felt both haunted and hunted.

One of my sons went on to marry a woman whose grandfather, like

Gerhard's father, had fought on the Eastern Front. Gerhard's father had not embraced National Socialism; my daughter-in-law's grandfather had, and ironically my daughter-in-law became a thoughtful, liberal, practicing Jew and was raising a Jewish son, my grandson. But with her mother, Germany and the *Shoah* were taboo. Bring up the subject, and this woman equated her own wartime suffering with the fate of the Jews, which seemed to me misguided. The importance of studying the *Shoah* was not to compare victimhood, but to continue wrestling with moral questions that arise out of that horrible past.

I asked myself if Gerhard was anti-Semitic, if I was anti-German. These were labels to resist. Gerhard had a point; judging was not the answer.

❧

Leaving Gerhard's, I walked toward the clock tower. On my right, *la savonnerie*, the soap shop. Inside, I strolled among honeycombed shelves filled with bars of soaps and tables displaying soap pyramids, their scents mingling, lavender, lime, lemon, vanilla. I brought a bar of soap to my nose and breathed in the scent of peach. Now bergamot, next apple, then cinnamon. There were vials of fragrant oils and diffusers, incense and jewelry. A short woman sat behind a tall, dark, wooden counter. If I hadn't known she would be there, was always there, I would have thought I was alone. Whenever I entered this shop, sometimes to browse, other times to buy, she sat as if in hiding. She did not greet me, had never greeted me, nor had I heard her greet other customers, and long ago I'd decided she was not simply unfriendly, but a grouch.

I held a dangling earring to my ear, looked in a mirror, turned my head left, then right. I was not shopping for earrings; I wanted to linger and feel Adèle in these walls. Like Gerhard, I wanted to mark Adèle's life with a plaque outside this shop in order to honor not her death, but her life. I fingered a necklace. Another pair of earrings. The woman stood as if to signal me, and so I carried a bar of lavender soap to the counter. Wordlessly, she took my money, then slipped my soap into a nearly flat brown paper bag the size of a maple leaf. I had the feeling that if Gerhard were to approach her about a plaque, she would shake her head. No, no plaque.

Plaques, though, were common practice throughout both France and Germany, so many plaques in Paris, particularly in the Marais. In German cities such as Cologne and Hamburg, the sculptor Gunter Demnig embedded *stolperstein*, stumbling blocks, shiny copper squares, into sidewalks, each square engraved with the name of a Jew who had been dragged away and murdered. Because each stone rose above the pavement, you stumbled, you noticed, you read: *Here lived.... Here worked....*

Standing outside *la savonnerie*, I took in the façade with its wide French doors and sash painted the same turquoise as the shutters. With the shutters opened and fastened to the outside of the building, there was no room for a plaque. Why not a *stolperstein*? But Auvillar did not want to stumble over its past. I thought about Adèle, a teenager as my two older granddaughters were teenagers. Adèle living in the flat above, Adèle a child of war, my granddaughters children of relative peace and relative prosperity, walking to school, laughing with friends, selfish in the way of teenaged girls. My granddaughters did not glance back into time. Who would lead them there? Perhaps they would have to stumble on their own to learn that the moral dilemmas of the *Shoah* are ongoing.

I stood outside the *tabac* and imagined Adèle spinning a rack with postcards. Every day the cards were the same. Still, she spun as if seeing this village for the first time, the Church of Saint Peter golden in sunlight, the stone pillars and red-tiled roof of the round market, the ancient chapel of Saint Catherine in the Old Port. Adèle spoke perfect unaccented French, and she wrote in French. She could have passed, but, really, in those days could anyone pass? How much time did she have? Three weeks? Two?

Inside the *tabac*, Adèle handed her postcards to the proprietor. Later, in her family's rooms above the soap shop, she would write to Hanna Papanek, her old school friend who had emigrated to the States. As the proprietor slipped Adèle's postcards into a paper bag, the proprietor's daughter, sitting on a stool behind the counter, stared in that uncompromising way of children, and that was why years and years later she would remember and say to Gerhard, "She used to come to my mother's shop. She bought postcards. She had beautiful hair."

Late that afternoon, as the sun dropped behind hills and trees, I carried a glass of wine to a picnic table beside the Garonne. Time circled and light faded like a blue note wailing. I watched the river's smooth surface and understood that, beneath that placid exterior, a strong current pulled. Adèle used to come here. She might have even sketched here. Adèle had dreamed of designing women's fashions. I'd seen her drawings wrapped in protective tissue when Pascal Caïla unpacked the family's suitcases — a woman in profile wearing a black gown, two girls wearing shorts and tight-fitting tops. In her own hand, Adèle had captioned this drawing in English: "*Hip, Hip, Hooray.*"

On the Kurzweil family's last night, Bruno Kurzweil sat at a table, composing a letter to a friend. He wrote, "I am anxious about my family. I feel problems coming."

Perhaps Adèle lay awake in her bed. Perhaps she padded into the parlor and looked over her father's shoulder before he covered his writing with his palm or a blotter. Perhaps they heard it at the same time, the sound of a motor coming closer.

Downstairs in front of the soap shop, gendarmes herded Bruno, Gisèle and Adèle Kurzweil up into the back of an open truck, the kind of truck a farmer would use to transport animals. Were the other three families already inside? Were the Kurzweils the first, the second, the last? Each person carried a small bundle, all that was allowed. The Kurzweil suitcases, packed so carefully for travel, stayed behind. In addition to the Kurzweils, the families were: Regina and Manfred Moriz, Liselotte and Bernard Roth, Sigismond and Anna Winewiez, Ernst Weisselberg and a son whose name was missing. There were five families, not four.

As dawn streaked its colors above the horizon and farmers made their way to barns and fields, the truck motored past, and I wondered if anyone had turned to look, or maybe refused to?

Seven months earlier at the Wannsee Conference in a suburb of Berlin, the Third Reich had ordered implementation of the Final Solution, ie. murder of all Jews. The families from Auvillar were taken to Septfonds, an internment camp outside of Montauban, then to Drancy. Bruno, Gisèle and Adèle Kurzweil joined convoy Number 30, and, on arrival at Auschwitz, all three were gassed.

🖎

The next day, back inside Gerhard's house, light was sparse under low ceilings. On the other side of the narrow high window, leaves clung to a spindly tree branch. A look of melancholy dimmed Gerhard's eyes. "Humanity is able to do anything, eh? Now, people in Europe are anti-Islam. We need to dialogue with all religions. With our commemoration, we had one intention. We did not want to point out past mistakes…"

Mistake was a word like accident. Mistakes were blunders, miscalculations, oversights, all slight, and off-the-mark, terms for what had happened in Auvillar. Better words were betrayal and moral ineptitude. Again, I bit my tongue. I was grateful for Gerhard's compassion and for his work to bring the past into the present.

I thought of that day Priscilla and I had biked to Moissac. We didn't have time to search for the secret house, so I'd returned on my own. I didn't find the house, but I found a wall with a plaque honoring Shatta and Simon Boulé — Shatta, sister to Sigismond Hirsch. Like *la colonie*, the *Eclaireurs Israèlites de France*, Jewish Scouts, ran the house in Moissac. *La colonie* housed girls; the house in Moissac housed boys. In Moissac, when German orders arrived announcing a raid, the mayor sent word to the Boulés. Forewarned, Shatta and Simon escorted the children to temporary shelter, as had Madame Gordin. Why in Moissac and not here in my beloved village of Auvillar?

"There is not a rational answer to be given about why one village is better than another," Gerhard said. "Here people helped, too. The Ursulines helped."

Ah, yes, the Ursulines, who sheltered Jean Hirsch.

"In this region, we can be proud. We have people who helped. The archbishops of Montauban and Toulouse helped. In our selection of speakers for this day of commemoration, we wanted to point out positive things. We wanted to make a memory of these families."

Accepting a terrible past was not the same as accepting guilt, but often it felt the same. I understood Gerhard's point. I asked about plaques. Gerhard shook his head. "It is too early."

"Seventy years and it's still too early?"

Gerhard wanted those plaques as much as I did, but he understood not only the mayor and his council, but the villagers. On the day of commemoration, the mayor and Pascal Caïla spoke. All events took place inside the Chapel of Saint Catherine in the Old Port. "Afterward, we walked to the bridge," Gerhard said. "We threw roses. It was very nice. Very good for young people. But we are not yet finished."

The plaques.

Later, at the river, I sat at my favorite picnic table. A cool breeze blew. Finally, clouds had given in to sun. I closed my eyes and lifted my chin to the warmth of the last rays. Something landed beside me on the bench and my eyes blinked open. I laughed. My neighbor's dog, the dachshund mix, sat beside me, his haunch touching my hip. I scratched behind the dog's ear. *"Bonjour. Ça va?"*

In the distance, my neighbor waved and called to the dog. He jumped down and they walked, woman and dog, along the grassy path that followed the river, the dog bounding ahead and then doubling back.

Adèle had sat here, not on this bench, not at this table, but here at the river. She breathed; she lived. She dreamed. She hoped and she sketched. Auvillar buried her story and years later, Gerhard found it and hoisted it up into the light of an August day of commemoration. I imagined Gerhard and Mary Jo leading the villagers from the chapel. They approached the blue suspension bridge and walked along the narrow sidewalk. At the railing, Gerhard lifted an arm as if to give the downbeat. The villagers dropped roses to the river below, long-stemmed pink and red roses, fragrant, fragile roses drifting down, then floating. The river swallowed them. Life was like that — fragile, beautiful and brutal. The villagers did not see her, but she was there, Adèle floating above them, wind sweeping her beautiful hair.

13

Eyes half-closed, Germaine said, softly. "I was *tourment*."
Pained and worried. Suffering.

Once again, I was visiting Germaine in her flat. I'd taken the TGV from Agen to Paris, and I was staying in my hotel in the Marais, greeted warmly by Catherine, one of the managers. Valerie met me there. We walked in the rain to Châtelet, rode the RER to Fontaine Michelon, our stop for Massy Palaiseau, and then splashed through puddles up the hill to Germaine's apartment complex, arriving breathless, our feet soaked. Our hair, too, in spite of umbrellas. "Ooh la, la," Germaine had said when she saw us.

I had just a few days in Paris before heading back to the States, and I needed to fit these interviews into Valerie's schedule. Cancelling was out of the question.

Over time, it had become increasingly clear to me that Vichy had not ended with Hitler's defeat. The complexities of who did what, where, and when spilled out and were still spilling into the present and future.

As I dug deeper into the larger story of post-war France, I discovered that in August, 1944, when forces of the French Liberation

Army entered Paris before the Allies, it was because French generals had insisted on being there first. They would liberate their home city. Allied generals gave in. Once both the French and the Allies had gained control, the Allies left to fight their way to Berlin. On May 8, 1945, nine months after the liberation of Paris, Germany surrendered, and the War in Europe was over. Jews came out of hiding. Refugees and prisoners trickled back. Most, however, ended up in DP (Displaced Persons) camps on either French or German soil. Months passed. A year passed before Germaine left Beaulieu-sur-Dordogne and returned to her home city.

Paris was like a giant beast emerging from a cave, stretching its neck, lifting its head and breathing the stink of collaboration, betrayal, deportation, and death. Cobblestones held the imprint of Nazi boots, and prison walls remembered prisoners' screams. Hardly a Jew was left alive. Correct that. Hardly, a foreign Jew was left alive. French Jews, those who had managed to go into hiding, surfaced to find their businesses and their flats in the hands of others. Their possessions were gone, dishes, pots, pans, furniture, clothes. Jews returning from the south faced the same losses.

Refugee organizations took over hotels, and with help from the Jewish Scouts, Germaine found a room for herself and the children on the rue Le Marois in the Sixteenth Arrondissment. Ever flexible to the needs of their people, the Jewish Scouts ran schools for Jewish orphans and prepared these children to make *Aliyah*, return to the homeland, which at that time was Palestine. Monsieur and Madame Gordin directed one of these schools, and once again, Madame hired Germaine to teach music. The school was in the Marais, and Germaine pedaled her bicycle across half the city to get there.

Today, as we spoke of those early post-war days, Germaine pushed the sleeves of her blue sweater to her elbows. She wore a long black skirt, a familiar silver pendant on a black cord at her neck. Seated in one of the apricot velvet chairs, she held onto the handle of her cane with both hands. Her gaze turned inward. "My husband came. He wanted to take the children to live with him in the east of France. He was living in a big house with his parents. They were wealthy. This was his condition for a divorce. I must give up the children. This I refused."

"He gave me nothing," Germaine said. "His father was a kind man. He sent me something every month." She earned another pittance teaching music. Ralph was asking for all she had left in this world to love: the children. Daniel was four, Aline, nearly three, and Arlette, the baby, not quite two.

I pictured a morning in spring. Chestnut trees in full bloom. On the sidewalk in front of the refugee hotel, Germaine straddled the low bar of her bicycle. All her possessions came from the generosity of others, clothing from the "Joint," American Jewish Joint Distribution Committee, her bicycle from the Rothschild Foundation. One day in the not-so-distant future, someone would steal her bicycle, and strangely Ralph, who was good with his hands, would find parts and build her another.

Arlette lifted her arms. Germaine hoisted her up and set her down inside a wicker basket fastened to the bicycle's handlebars. Then, Aline went into a basket on the back fender. Daniel sat on the seat between his mother's legs. Germaine pushed off. She rode through Paris's strangely empty streets, no cars, no buses, no taxis — no petrol. She thought of Ralph. He owned and drove a red car. Where did he find petrol?

She touched Daniel's hair. How he loved his father's red car, and whenever Ralph came to Paris — and he did come to badger Germaine to have the children stay with him — he took Daniel for a ride. Seeing them drive off, Germaine asked herself the same questions Ralph asked over and over. What kind of life was she giving the children? Would they be better off with their father? He had a house, a yard where they could play. He had money.

As she pedaled her three children through the streets, she noticed the absence of sound, no whoosh of buses, blare of taxi horns, shouts or whistles. The city had not been bombed, but toward the end of the war, the outskirts had — factories feeding the German war machine had burned and blanketed Paris with soot and ash. An acrid scent lingered. Paris's characteristic white limestone had blackened. Germaine missed the clean façades and clean statues. She missed the city's pulse. She swerved to avoid a pile of rubble. No one to take it away. She supposed she should be grateful to be here at all.

Before this war, Germaine had thought of herself as French, only French. She'd been engaged to marry a Catholic man and had little sense of a Jewish identity. Now, she thought of herself as both French and Jewish. In *la colonie*, she celebrated Shabbat and Hanukkah with the girls. "But I didn't feel comfortable with ritual," she said. "I always felt there was no God. What is God?"

She linked ritual to God. I did not. I linked ritual to community and continuity, the generations that preceded mine, the generations that would come after. Yet, I often asked the same question: "What is God?"

It wasn't easy to call yourself a Jew in post-war Paris where Jews reminded Parisians of all they wanted to forget: Occupation and Collaboration. Ashamed, confused and wondering what had gone wrong in their beloved city and their beloved country, Jews, too, wanted to forget. Most of the surviving Jews were French citizens, men and women who had believed in their land of *liberté, égalité, fraternité*; yet, their officials and gendarmes had compiled lists of names and handed them over to the Germans. Better not to dwell on these things. Germaine did not dwell, nor did she openly declare she was a Jew.

After an immediate, but brief crackdown, informers and collaborators blended into the mix of post-war life. No one spoke of past deeds; yet, all could breathe the suffering and guilt hanging in the air. Germaine did not want her children to feel like prey, and she made a conscious decision: she would not tell them they were Jews. Nor would she say they were Protestant or Catholic. It was as if she thought she could leave a blank space that no one would notice, not the outside world, not the children. Truth pressed at that empty space.

On that spring morning, Daniel leaned and gripped the handlebars of his mother's bicycle. Aline grabbed a hunk of her mother's skirt. Arlette, the baby, sat upright in her basket and held on. Germaine was speeding down a steep hill, wind whipping strands of hair across her cheek. She could not stop. The bicycle had no brakes. The street leveled and Germaine coasted to the entrance of the children's school, another relief agency enterprise. Here the children would eat two hot meals, breakfast and lunch, and for this Germaine was grateful. Daniel hopped down and steadied the bicycle. Germaine lifted Aline, then Arlette. The baby clung to Germaine's neck.

Now, alone on her bicycle, Germaine pedaled to the Marais.

I was struck by her strength and determination, the way she followed what Mama called that still small voice inside your heart. Mama used to say if I listened, I would hear that voice. Germaine described that voice as her Jiminy Cricket, a bird sitting on her shoulder and singing into her ear.

Post-war, money from Germaine's mother's family had dried up. Her father was broke. He couldn't find work. Finally, a brother gave him what Germaine described as "a small job." He also received a government pension, but it wasn't much. He could not help his daughter. "You must give the children to Ralph," her father said. Her mother agreed.

Germaine leaned and rested her hands on her knees. "I said to my parents, 'I am fine. I have everything under control.' Oh, Sandell, I was like a child, and all of life was like a game."

☙

I was in my late twenties, a mother of three, when life for me too, was like a game. I made the moves I needed to make, and that was how I got through each day, washing, drying and folding the family's clothes, preparing our meals and driving — to the supermarket, to nursery school, to play dates, then home with the baby strapped into his car seat beside me in the passenger's seat. At home, the boys and I built skyscrapers and parking garages with wooden blocks. We parked Matchbox cars inside. We played board games. I fed the dog, fed the boys, gave them baths and afterwards, we snuggled down on one of their single beds, all four of us, as I read them stories. It was the late '6os. The world was churning and burning. I was a suburban mother and wife, but I dressed as if I were a flower child, wearing stars and stripes jeans and peasant blouses and tying a narrow leather headband around my forehead. I worked part-time for my local newspaper covering the school news, and I attended staid school committee meetings in my hippie get-up. I didn't wear shoes, not even sandals. I'd already given up two careers, one as a dancer in New York City — the realization of a childhood dream — a second as a high school English teacher. I was searching for the woman I might have become, or perhaps searching for authenticity. That's what I thought the flower children had found, a way to be themselves.

I came home late after meetings, often not until well past eleven, to a quiet and sleeping house. I walked down the basement stairs to my "office" a table, a chair, a lamp, and a typewriter in a corner where I wrote my copy, then drove to town and slipped my story under the editor's door.

We were linked, Germaine and I, by our rebellious spirits and by our struggle, when young, to be both women and mothers. Independent and connected. I'd imagined for her an amped-up life with sharpened senses. I'd imagined lovers because that was something that over the years, I'd wanted to do and had not done. I figured wartime gave women permission to fly free. Instead, like me, she became a mother.

⚜

Germaine rolled her fists in front of her belly in a gesture of agitation. "I did not know what to do. What if my parents were correct?"

Creeping doubt.

"I was *tourment*."

That word, again. Troubled and anxious, but something more, a restlessness invading every cell in her body.

In the school in the Marais, Germaine poured out her troubles to Madame Gordin. Maybe at day's end, she stood at a window and looked down into a courtyard. She was tired. Soon, she would pedal to the children's school, then to her single room where every evening she warmed milk on a one-burner hot plate, offered the children bread and cheese, maybe jam if she was lucky. She'd wash them and get them ready for bed. She'd sing to them, kiss them, then settle down into bed beside them, all four snuggling like puppies. The children slept. Germaine lay awake. She could not go on like this.

She sank down into the cushions of a threadbare couch. Madame Gordin offered tea. Germaine held the cup with both hands and looked into Madame's eyes. She was nearly too tired to speak. Finally, she said, "Should I give up the children? I have nothing to give them, only my love."

Madame rested a hand on Germaine's arm and spoke softly. "You must find diversion. Something to take your mind from your troubles.

My husband is teaching a course in Jewish philosophy. The school is not far from your hotel. I will tell him you are coming."

Germaine shifted, anger seeping into her melancholy. What did she want with Jewish philosophy? She was not an *intello*, an intellectual.

"Go," Madame said.

At the school, also run by a Jewish refugee organization, she stood in an open doorway and surveyed the classroom. "I didn't see a single seat. I said to myself, 'Good, I can go home and tell Madame I tried,'" Germaine said.

Just then, a man beckoned. Germaine entered and sat down beside him. He was short and slight of build. Not her type. Germaine liked tall, athletic men like Ralph. He introduced himself and made small talk.

"I don't know why, but I found his accent charming. The next day, I asked Madame, 'Who is this Léon Poliakov?'"

"Ah. Léon Poliakov. *Très intéressant. Très compliqué,*" Madame had said.

During the War, Léon Poliakov and Monsieur Gordin had worked to save Jewish refugee children, and in order to pass as a Frenchman, he'd spoken perfect unaccented French. Now, he was speaking French like a Russian, again. He was an historian, a brilliant man, but he had troubles. "He is engaged to marry, but his fiancée is very religious, and he is secular," Madame said. "He did not think this would matter. Now, it mattered. Also, he is seeing a second woman. I did not know he would be taking that class. I don't know if I would have sent you."

When Léon telephoned, he was clear, an affair nothing more. Germaine, too, was clear. "You know, I have three children."

"What does that matter?"

To most men, that would matter.

On their first date, they walked along the Avenue de Versailles,

Léon slight of build, Germaine sturdy, broad-shouldered and matching his height. Léon talked about testimonies he had collected during and immediately after the War. He'd translated the archives of the Gestapo and was accompanying the French delegation to Nuremberg. Under Vichy, he'd been a hunted man. Now, the hunted was the hunter. Although he would become known for his work, at this moment his future was not assured.

In spite of his words on the telephone, there was no affair. Léon did not wish to take on a third sexual liaison. Night after night, they walked and Germaine listened as Léon talked because this was what he did, talk and talk. Germaine didn't mind. She was happy. Although, this was not the diversion Madame Gordin had intended, Germaine's spirits lifted. Now, sitting opposite me, Germaine said, "From the beginning, we were very, very good together."

Léon broke with both his fiancée and his lover. He rented a flat in the Thirteenth Arrondissement for Germaine and the children. The Thirteenth was a hilly working-class district with narrow cobbled streets. During the Occupation, members of the Resistance had sheltered here, perhaps Léon himself. Soon, Léon gave up his own flat and moved in with them. As Germaine told me this story, I remained calm, but I wanted to shout: *He moved in? In the forties? Amazing. What about your parents? What about Ralph? What about you? So brave.*

When the school in the Marais closed, Germaine took on private pupils. She found work as a choir leader. "Moi, je travaille," Germaine said. Always, she worked. She took classes and studied music. Evenings, she attended concerts. Because Léon researched and wrote at home, he became the at-home parent, present but not engaged. After school, when the children returned to the flat, he did not hear their shouts or their fights, and mostly, they were on their own. Still, he loved them and called them *l'equipe*, the team. When they cried, he offered his hands palms up. "Give me your tears. I am the king of tears."

Léon filled the flat with his friends, all trying to make sense of the genocide they'd managed to live through. One of those men was Romain Gary, novelist, filmmaker and World War II aviator.

In *Promise at Dawn*, Gary's memoir, he claims that when he was a child and too young to understand evil, he intuited evil, and he named the evil gods — Stupidity, "with his scarlet monkey's behind, the swollen head of a doctrinaire and a passionate love for abstractions; he has always been the Germans' pet...." Next, Absolute Truth and Total Righteousness, "the lord of all true believers and bigots; whip in hand.... one half of the human race licks his boots." Now, the God of Mediocrity, "one of the most powerful of the gods, and the most eagerly listened to; he is to be found in every political camp, from right to left, lurking behind every cause, every ideal, always present, rubbing his hands whenever a dream of human dignity is stamped into the mud." And finally, "the god of Acceptance and Servility, of survival at all costs... He knows how to worm his way into a tired heart... appears before you when it is so easy to give up and to remain alive takes only a little cowardice."

Hardly a child's thoughts, but thoughts I pondered. I would never know what I would have done had I been faced with Germaine's circumstance or what I would have done at the war's end, rejected my identity or embraced it? I thought of the years I'd decorated a Christmas tree and hung a wreath on my front door, refusing to announce to the world that I was a Jew. I hid my difference and shrank inside when I saw photographs in the newspaper of swastikas painted on synagogue walls or when I heard references to Jew York City, Jew Town, Jew Street or a friend's casual remark: "He Jewed me down."

Others who congregated in Germaine's and Léon's flat were Jacques Attali, economist and writer; Maxime Rodinson, Marxist historian and socialist; Stéphane Hessel, Léon's nephew, diplomat, writer and years and years later, the inspiration for Occupy Wall Street. As time passed, Léon would break with Hessel over Hessel's comparison of the Israeli occupation of Palestinian lands to the Nazi Occupation of France. Hessel would be forced to clarify, saying he saw no parallel between the horrors of Nazism and the illegal attitude of the state of Israel, but the damage had been done. Léon was not satisfied.

Léon's research papers and his books — with their heady discussions of anti-Semitism and National Socialism — filled the flat. Yet, neither Germaine nor Léon spoke of the war or the fate of the Jews with the children. Neither mentioned the camps. These horrors, they believed, were not for a child's ears. Nor was the fact that Germaine's and Ralph's children were Jews. But wherever secrets lie buried, their vapor escapes.

Evenings, when Léon's friends visited, Germaine would cook a fish stew, heavy on potatoes, light on fish. She would prepare a salad with whatever fresh vegetables she could find at the market. She did not consider her time in the kitchen subservient. Germaine loved to cook, and her kitchen was fragrant with spice — oregano and mint, cinnamon and clove, spices that Yvonne had learned to love when Germaine cooked for the girls in *la colonie*, spices that harkened back to her mother's and father's life in Turkey long ago.

Always, Germaine joined Léon and his friends at the table. Her life was with Léon; yet, she was married to Ralph. She was married and not married. Free and tethered. She was my mother's contemporary and she dared to live openly with a man who was not her husband. She claimed her place and her space.

Finally, because *he* wanted to marry, Ralph asked for a divorce. Daniel, seven, chose to live with his father. Why had Germaine and Ralph given this weighty decision to a child? When I asked, Germaine's eyes clouded over. Probably I'd asked the same question she'd been asking herself for decades. She didn't know. "He was seven and he went. His father had a red car. Maybe he wanted to ride in a red car. Maybe I didn't love him enough. I don't know, Sandell. I don't know."

Daniel visited Germaine during school vacations and for most of every summer. Still, her heart was broken.

In 1952, she and Léon married. They had little money. "The wedding rings were not made of gold," Germaine said. "It was a mixture." In 1960, when Germaine was nearly forty-two and Léon was almost fifty, Germaine gave birth to a second son, Jean Michael. By then, Germaine and Léon had moved to this flat in Massy Palaiseau where we sat. When Jean Michael was three, he wanted to fly, so he climbed out onto the balcony with its pots of blooming geranium and up onto the railing, glistening now in the rain. I imagined three-year-old Jean Michael, spreading his arms and jumping into the air. "He had nothing," Germaine said. "Nothing."

No broken bones, no bruises, no concussion. A branch or a bush must have broken his fall. That night Léon walked to the synagogue, but he did not go inside. "He walked around outside," Germaine said. I supposed, in this way, he thanked the God he didn't believe in for his son's life. Strangely and for no reason, I can imagine myself doing the same thing, honoring mystery.

In the room that used to be Léon's study, Germaine sifted through a stack of her artwork. In addition to her other pursuits, she dried flowers, painted them, and assembled the painted flowers into collages. If I were to develop a theory on aging, I would say that those who created lived, if not longer lives, then, more fulfilling lives. Germaine wanted to give me a gift to take home to the States. I was leaving the next day. By then, we both knew I'd return. I protested. She insisted. Together, we chose a collage. "Will you frame it?" Germaine said.

14

Three years had passed since my first visit to Auvillar, and I'd been awarded a second Fellowship at Moulin à Nef. Again, I was staying at the MV, *Maison Vielhescazes*. One brilliantly sunny fall day, Robert pulled his twelve-year-old silver Mercedes up to the curb and I climbed inside. We picked up Gerhard in the village and drove into the countryside.

I had been wrong about the house in the village. The Gestapo did not arrest Sigismond and Berthe Hirsch at *numéro trois place des halles*; they arrested them in Saint Michel, a petite village in the township of Auvillar, about three and a half miles south of this village, and that was where we were headed. Finally, in a recent interview, Gerhard had told me about a large château, then added, "Not many people know of this place."

A secret.

We stood on a corner outside a fire-engine-red iron fence with posts that ended in spear points. No cars passed on the road and, except for this property with its wide expanse of lawn and its impressive château, all of the other houses sat close to a narrow sidewalk and the street.

This was so typical in the French countryside, a large château, signifier of wealth and class, surrounded by modest houses and farmland. And, always, these châteaux were walled or fenced.

A white stone arch framed a massive red door with a fanlight above. Red iron spears repeating the fence motif formed the glazing bars. All other windows were shuttered tight. How could this mansion have been the family's wartime residence? Had Sigismond paid for this place himself? Had the Resistance paid? The Jewish Scouts? I checked with Gerhard. "They lived here?"

Gerhard moved his large head slowly. "Yes, here. I must get the key. She is expecting me."

A neighbor across the street.

I photographed the distant château. I photographed the iron fence. Later when I looked at the photo I noticed a missing spear head in the fence.

Robert paced. Gerhard returned. "She said to me she would be at home. Without the key, we cannot go inside."

"But we can see the garden," I said. I touched the gate and it gave way.

"No, no," Robert said. He rested a palm on my arm.

"Why not?" I asked.

"I am reluctant to do this," Gerhard said. "There are new owners. I took contacts with the old owners." He took contacts; he knew them. "I do not know these new people."

"But you know the spot, the place in the garden where the Gestapo arrested them?"

"Yes, yes, I know."

I turned to look over my shoulder. The narrow sidewalks were empty. I listened to the buzz of stillness in the air before I pushed open the gate and stepped inside. What could anyone do, ask us to leave? Again, Robert's hand rested on my arm.

"We mustn't," Gerhard said.

Just as I stepped back, two women rounded the back corner of the château, one older, one younger. At first I thought they were mother and daughter. Perhaps, though, they were friends out for a stroll with their dogs, one dog an old retriever, the other a feisty black French bulldog that stiffened its legs, held its ground, and barked. The younger woman spoke harshly to the barking dog. Turning quickly, the dog ran off, and now, out of her reach, the animal took his stiff-legged stance and gave her a look as if to say, back off, I'm doing my job. All eyed us warily, dogs and women. Robert lifted his thumb to the narrow brim of his cap and, in an old-fashioned gentlemanly gesture, greeted them both. "You are connected here with the château?" he asked.

The older woman smiled. "We have permission to walk with the dogs. There are paths."

"Yes, yes," Gerhard said. "I know these paths. I have been here before. I have permission from the old owners, but I do not know these new people."

The women had not met these new people, either. They were taking their permission from the people they knew. Each gave that French moue, as if to say that, for the moment, these new people did not matter. I was surrounded by the cadence of French, words drifting like fuzzy milkweed seeds. I caught a few words and understood my friends were explaining who I was, a visitor from the States with an historical interest in this property. A discussion ensued as to where the woman across the street might have gone, perhaps to visit her daughter or call on a friend.

"So, it will be all right with you if we enter and walk around?" Robert said.

The older woman stepped back from the gate and bid us enter. After the women and their dogs left, Gerhard carefully closed the gate. It appeared locked.

Thin clouds drifted across a true-blue sky, casting shadows on the lawn. It was late in October and I wondered if this would be the last day of brilliant sun and near-summer warmth before autumn would insinuate its way into the air. I walked to the edge of the lawn where a pomegranate tree bore fruit so ripe the skins had burst, exposing a myriad of seeds all stuck together in a viscous liquid, like fish eggs. I backed up to take a photo, then went closer. In my photograph the seeds are blurry, slick, and orangey-red, as if alive.

In Jewish lore, a pomegranate has six hundred and thirteen seeds, the number of *mitzvot* in *Torah*. *Mitzvot*, commandments or good deeds, all six hundred and thirteen summed up in these words by the ancient sage Hillel: *What is hateful to you, do not do to another.*

This is different from *Do unto others what you would have them do unto you.* Hillel asks each of us to consider what is hateful to us and, in doing so, speaks to our essence. If we are just and ethical, then we can do what is right. I liked to think of myself as a just and ethical person, but I had never truly been tested. I wondered. I mulled. Had I been an adult living through those terrible times, what kind of person would I have been? What kind of person would I have become?

I touched a leaf and thought about picking a pomegranate, but one transgression, trespassing, was enough.

Behind the château, Robert climbed stairs and leaned over a balcony. Just as I looked up, he snapped my picture. Robert climbed down and, without speaking, walked to an archway where a single red rose clung to a trellis. Like Robert, I was taken with this tenacious flower. Together we snapped photos, but Robert had the true photographer's eye, moving in closer and closer.

In a corner, where the main part of the château met a wing, ivy grew at the base of a brick cistern before climbing a wall. A rusty-red iron water pump with a sloping handle stood like a sculpture, its cylinder swelling into the bulbous shape of an urn. On the bulb, a lion's head with a molded mane and a mouth ready to spill water. Attached to the sides of the urn, filigreed ironwork formed a heart. I wondered if this was the last thing Berthe and Sigismond Hirsch saw before the Gestapo's flashlights blinded them.

The air was quiet here, the silence holy. I stood in front of a box-wood hedge. Wild cyclamen bloomed in the grass. Robert and I photographed the cyclamen blooms the size of violets. We photographed trees and then, we focused on a single tree, admiring its shape, its branches, its textures, and its grooves. This tree had needles, not leaves, and I thought of Priscilla and our walk along the *Chemin*. We'd seen a tree like this one, a *cedrus lebani*, Cedar of Lebanon. In biblical times, David built his palace with wood from the Cedar of Lebanon. Solomon built both his palace and the temple with this wood. I felt as if I'd entered an ancient site, one layered with time and memory.

⤝

On that day in 1943 no one wanted to go inside, not Sigismond or Berthe, who carried the baby Nicole in her arms. Not Jean, not the Hirsches' friends Monsieur and Madame Latig. Perhaps, though, Berthe did not carry Nicole. Perhaps the baby was inside, napping in her crib. Perhaps Jean, too, had stayed indoors or followed one of the paths to the river. Madame Latig had come to give Jean lessons, but the day was too beautiful for lessons. No one knew for sure the sequence of events. In his testimony on the AJPN website, Jean Hirsch told one story. Odette told another.

Odette lived at *numéro quatre place des halles* and, at eighty-three, she ran a gîte, making beds, cleaning rooms, and preparing breakfast for her guests. According to Gerhard, she'd been Sigismond Hirsch's housekeeper. Odette was a petite woman with stark white hair. I'd seen her in the village pushing a heavy wheelbarrow filled with kindling and cord wood along cobbled streets. Each time, she'd worn a housedress, the kind that wrapped and tied over a dress, along with thick flesh-colored stockings and sensible shoes. She had a no-nonsense way about her and she seemed to me the epitome of strength. If you were old and you lived in Auvillar, you climbed hills and, if necessary, you pushed a heavy wheelbarrow through narrow cobbled streets.

We'd met and spoken in her parlor, with Gerhard as my interpreter. For five years, Odette had kept house for Sigismond Hirsch in Auvillar, and often she traveled to Maurepas, Sigismond's residence outside of Paris, to keep house for him there. Pictures on the internet showed me a grand stucco structure with clean modern lines, pointed gabled roofs, and a myriad of windows. Jean, a physician too, had built the house for his father. When Odette traveled to Maurepas she stayed for a month, sometimes longer. Maurice, her husband, now deceased — not to be confused with Yvonne's Uncle Maurice — did not like her long absences, but he tolerated them. Rumor in the village linked Odette's husband to the resistance. Rumor also linked him to Jewish ancestry. "No. Not Jewish," Odette said.

She did not deny a relationship with the resistance. Nor did she affirm one. But I supposed a deep and unspoken connection among the three, Odette, Maurice, and Sigismond Hirsch.

On that fateful October afternoon, when Sigismond and Berthe finally went indoors, they sent Jean home with the Latigs, saying he must finish his lessons, and that was why, Odette said, he was not at home that evening when the Gestapo burst into the kitchen. She knew nothing about a piano lesson and a priest. But she did say the château was a gathering place for the Resistance and, on that night, two resistance workers had arrived to collect false identity papers and false passports. However, the Gestapo were only interested in Sigismond and Berthe Hirsch. Odette knew this for a fact. The agents arrested no one else.

I imagined them sitting at a kitchen table, Sigismond, Berthe, and the resistance fighters, all planning strategy when they heard the sound of a motor. Why hadn't the dog barked? According to Odette, the dog had run away. Cars were rare in Saint Michel, particularly in wartime. Sensing danger, Berthe and Sigismond ran outside.

Odette said there were many versions of what happened to the baby that night. One story said one of the Resistance handed Nicole out a window and into the arms of a neighbor. Another said no one knew exactly how the infant was saved, but the next day Madame Chambord, a baker's wife, took Nicole to a château in Le Pin, a neighboring village. Still another said that Shatta Simon arrived from Moissac to take both children, Jean and Nicole. All these stories contradicted Jean Hirsch's story of being met on the road by resistance workers as he walked home the next morning. How accurately we professed to remember. How faulty our memory. Beyond memory there is story, human action and interaction, cause and effect, and some mysterious connection we feel but cannot name.

I heard the sound of a helicopter and looked up. Not a helicopter, a small prop plane flying high. Gerhard looked, too. Now, lowering his gaze, he pointed to a clump of bushes with branches hanging low. "Here," he said. "Here is where they were arrested. Here is where the Gestapo found them."

I did not take a photograph. This site was holy, a sanctuary, an altar. Was my reluctance to take a photo a vestige of the Jewish prohibition against displaying images in a sanctuary? We make no images of God. We bury our dead in simple shrouds and unadorned pine coffins. We carry no flowers to graves. Instead, we pile pebbles on a headstone and, in this way, each of us says, I have been here and I remember you. Robert did not take pictures either and so we stood, all three silent, with our heads bowed. Were we praying? Probably, each in his or her own way.

A bird alighted on a branch. Then another. The branch shivered and I felt as if the spirits of Berthe and Sigismond were not alone in this place.

We idled back the way we had come. Outside the gate, we climbed into Robert's old gray Mercedes and took our usual seats. Robert drove slowly, as if to give each of us time to absorb the haunting nature of this day. We motored past Saint Michel's deserted sidewalks and the one hotel that had closed until spring. Even the church doors were shut tight. As the road curved, the sun blazed. In that instant, I could see them, Berthe and Sigismond Hirsch crouched beneath a bush, Gestapo agents shining their blinding lights.

That night at dinner at Moulin à Nef, Mary Jo maneuvered me away from the group just as Cheryl was asking us to take our seats. I followed her to a narrow corridor outside the kitchen. She glanced over her shoulder. Satisfied no one was listening, she spoke. "I have had a phone call from the owner of the property where you went with Gerhard. He is worried concerning the history of this house and with the photographs you have taken. He wants to see what you will write."

I stiffened. "I don't know if I will write anything."

"But if you do..." Her voice dropped off. Clearly, she had read my displeasure. "I don't have his number with me, but if you stop by tomorrow I will give it to you and you can call. This history is difficult for people."

I let her words drop down into an imaginary bucket. I had no intention of stopping by or of calling the owner. I'm sure she knew this. I thought of the two women with their dogs and of the caretaker who was not at home. Word traveled in these villages. I wondered why the new owner would care about me, an American writing in a language he didn't understand for people he did not know. I answered my own question: because he refused to face this history.

As I approached the table, Cheryl motioned to an empty chair beside Gerhard. She seated Mary Jo at the far end of the table. Mary Jo and I would not share dinner conversation. Intentional? Gerhard spoke to me of a concert in the abbey in Moissac that coming Sunday. "We are sponsoring this." His and Mary Jo's *Société Auvillaraise Culturelle Fran-co-Allemande*. "A young man is playing. He is a very talented pianist. I think you would enjoy this concert."

Except for my writing, which I did religiously, I did not plan. "Maybe," I said. Then, "Thank you."

"There is no rush. We will go anyway. You can call."

Cheryl ladled pumpkin soup and Gerhard passed me a bowl. We were ten at the table, and Robert sat across from me. He looked intently into his soup, and I remembered that he could not smell the aromas of cinnamon and nutmeg, and so he observed texture and color. Now that we were all served, Cheryl dipped her spoon, indicating we might taste. The soup was spicy and sweet, a deep pumpkin color with pomegranate seeds sprinkled on top. Robert spooned up soup and seeds. He gave me a look as if to remind me of the pomegranate tree in San Michel and a secret he, Gerhard, and I shared. Our afternoon was not table talk.

"The pumpkin comes from our neighbor's garden," Cheryl said. "This may be the last. He says he's getting too old."

"And the pomegranate seeds?" I asked.

"Oh, a tree on the road."

Gerhard held a basket with slices of baguette and, as I reached, he leaned toward me. "The owner of the château has called. He is concerned with our visit."

"So Mary Jo said."

"She is maybe a little troubled, but I wouldn't worry."

I tore my hunk of baguette. "I'm not."

Both lie and truth. I knew how to will worry away.

As courses appeared and disappeared, talk ranged from music to art to politics. Robert refilled my wine glass. As with most meals here, we stayed long at the table. Two-hour dinners were not uncommon.

When finally we rose, Mary Jo made her way toward me. "All through dinner, I have been thinking of the arrest. Did you see the photographs of Berthe? There are two."

In the first, Berthe is a vibrant young woman with full cheeks and a sweet smile, looking confidently into the camera's lens. In the second, her cheeks have hollowed and she has grown old.

Mary Jo shook her head. "I cannot understand what went wrong that night."

I answered quickly. "A captain in the Vichy forces turned them in."

"Yes, but who told *him*?"

An informant. Why hadn't I thought of that?

Robert turned. "I could not help listening. It is significant between people — who stays inside the château and who stays in a small house outside, eh?"

Borders. Barriers. Walls. Before the war, no Jew would have or could have lived in such a grand château. Before the war, no Jews had lived in any of these villages.

The Gestapo transported Berthe and Sigismond Hirsch to a prison in Toulouse. After torturing Sigismond, they shipped them both to Drancy. On November 20, 1943, Sigismond and Berthe Hirsch became part of Convoy 62 bound for Auschwitz. Berthe, thirty-seven, was gassed on arrival. Sigismond, also thirty-seven, was sent to work with Mengele.

15

To find one's way after Auschwitz, to find one's soul, to find a life — how did a person begin?

Probably it was Dr. Josef Mengele himself who sent Berthe Hirsch to the gas chamber. Probably it was Mengele who handpicked Sigismond to work with him in his clinic. Mengele had a particular interest in research into twins, a popular field in the early forties when researchers were trying to determine whether certain factors were hereditary or environmental. As the masses arrived, Mengele searched the emptying cattle cars selecting Jewish and Gypsy twins — mostly children — for his lethal, agonizing, cruel experiments. I thought of the eleven thousand children pictured on the lighted wall inside the *Mémorial de la Shoah* in Paris, their faces bright with life.

On the AJPN website, Jean Hirsch wrote that his father read x-rays during the war. Perhaps this was true. Perhaps this was what he needed to believe so that he would not share his father's haunted dreams. According to my research, however, doctors who worked with Mengele performed more grisly tasks. They also carried out autopsies on their victims.

Freed by the Americans in May 1945, Sigismond Hirsch spent time in a resettlement camp before returning to Paris and once again practicing medicine. Ironically, Yvonne Lieser was one of his patients. "He experimented on women," Yvonne said to me one day. She'd learned of his work with Mengele. Perhaps, this was well-known among French Jews who had one way or another survived the war.

I blurted. "And you still went to see him?"

She shrugged as if to say, *you are an American, what do you know of these things?*

In 1951, Sigismond Hirsch returned to Auvillar and began buying houses. Villagers sold their houses reluctantly. They had not recovered from the war — so many men shipped to Germany for forced labor, so many imprisoned there. Not all returned. If folks were poor before the war, they were worse off after. Farms were in ruins, livestock long gone, machinery was old, and petrol rationed — not that anyone could afford to buy it. Add to that the complications of Occupation, collaboration, secrecy, rumor, innuendo and distrust.

Young people were leaving to look for opportunity elsewhere. Then, malls came to France as they had in the States, taking commerce from village centers. Storefronts sat empty. Old people died. Babies were not born. In Auvillar, "For Sale" signs cropped up like dandelions.

Once again, I sat at Gerhard's table. Once again, he poured coffee. "Sigismond Hirsch owned maybe thirteen or fifteen houses, I am not sure," Gerhard said. "He had money from the German government."

Reparation money. I read about reparation payments made immediately after the war and in more recent times, agreements too complicated for me to unravel. I had only Gerhard's word as to the source of Hirsch's money. Reparation in German is *wivdergutmachen*, to rectify, to amend, to recompense, to atone, to make right, but how could any government compensate for a murdered wife, lost children, and those years spent working with Josef Mengele?

Villagers resented the source of Hirsch's money. Hadn't they suffered, too? Why all this fuss about the Jews? Always, the Jews. And what was Hirsch going to do with his houses? He couldn't live in them all.

"He had in mind to bring friends," Gerhard said. "They would come here on holiday. It was a good idea."

"A Jewish community?"

"I don't think so, but I am not sure."

I did think so. Community is embedded in Torah. All Jews, past, present, and future, stood and trembled at Mount Sinai the moment thunder rolled and lightning split the sky and Moses climbed down from the mountain holding the Torah in his arms. We are a timely and timeless people and, in a bizarre twist, I too would have belonged to Sigismond Hirsch's alliance of friends, my spirit traveling to foreign shores. This sense of community had in part compelled my research — ever since I learned a single name: Jean Hirsch.

Gerhard wanted me to deepen my understanding of Vichy in this area where both the Resistance and German occupation existed in tandem. Villagers ran risks from both sides. Families were caught in conflicting loyalties. People were suspicious, wary, poor, hungry. He told the story of Dunes, a hamlet like Saint Michel that was part of Auvillar. "There is bad history in Dunes," Gerhard said. It was November 1944. Two Italian women living nearby tipped off the SS about resistance in the village and, in reprisal, the Nazis marched seventy Frenchmen into the town square, picked twelve, and hanged them one by one. Folks understood the same could have happened in Auvillar's *centre-ville*. After the war, resistance fighters took the law into their own hands, formed a firing squad and executed the two women. Word was that one of them was still alive when they flung her into her grave. Luckily for her, they finished her off.

This was justice in the aftermath — execution without trial, brutality taking sway over rightfulness. Throughout France, women accused of taking German lovers found themselves seated on platforms in town squares surrounded by folks they'd lived with all of their lives. Their neighbors came to watch the spectacle. They brought their children. Fighters with machine guns patrolled. On a platform, barbers shaved each woman's head. This was France's *éxpuration sauvage*, savage purge.

I was in my early twenties, married and living in suburban Boston, when I first saw the film *Hiroshima Mon Amour*, directed by Alan Resnais and written by Marguerite Duras, that tells the story of a French movie actress living in occupied Nevers. The actress takes a German soldier as her lover. At Liberation, members of the Resistance shoot her lover before her eyes. They shave her head, shaming her and her family.

I must have repressed that particular memory, for as I researched Vichy France the subject struck me as new. Shaved heads, they did that? In France? I'd fallen into believing the guiding myth that the *Shoah* belonged first to Germany and, second, to Eastern Europe. Not to France. Never to France.

Resnais and Duras had gotten it right, but this was no film. This was life. There was nothing comparable for French men who had taken German women as their lovers.

In the camps, Nazis shaved the heads of Jews. If you were chosen for work, your head was shaved. If you were chosen for death, your head was shaved. A shaved head was a sign of humiliation, degradation and disgrace. Liberators of the camps found mounds of hair. Over the years, that hair turned gray. Hair sank into the earth and took its place among ancient coins, shards of pottery, bits of bone, and abandoned words. Folks start over and forget, but place remembers.

Gerhard and I left our coffee cups on the table. We stood outside his house, a light mist falling. I zipped my raincoat to my chin. Gerhard wore his tan jacket unzipped and his shirt collar open at the neck. He pointed up. "Do you see?"

I saw a shelf with a figure of a pilgrim attached to his house, announcing to all that he and Mary Jo ran a gîte and welcomed pilgrims. The figure, carved from wood and weather-worn, was dressed in a blue tunic, a white shirt with a collar, and a black wide-brimmed pilgrim's hat. He carried a walking stick and wore a scallop shell — proof that he had walked to Santiago del Compostela and back.

As for what I was supposed to see — the roof line of a house that Sigismond Hirsch had once owned, a house that Jean Hirsch had inherited and subsequently sold to Gerhard — well, I couldn't see that. Gerhard had broken through walls and added the Hirsch house to his. So much for Jean Hirsch's story of hardly knowing Gerhard Schneider. Now, looking up, I couldn't figure out where one house ended and another began, and that precisely had been the problem, roof tiles coming loose and causing leaks. Finally, Jean Hirsch agreed to repair the roof, but the workmanship was shoddy and water continued to leak into Gerhard's house. "What could I do?" Gerhard said. "I bought the house. The one house Sigismond Hirsch fixed up for himself is *numéro trois, place des halles*, next door to Odette, but you know this already."

The house with the beautiful wooden door and an opened window that I had looked through and into a garden where I'd imagined the family, Sigismond, Berthe, and Jean, all taking tea. I hadn't known then about Nicole. Now I pictured Sigismond Hirsch, an old man, opening those same shutters. He would see Gerhard in the plaza, motion to him, and invite him in. They would discuss philosophy. But Hirsch was anxious and irritable, Gerhard said. I couldn't imagine what festered in his body, his mind, his dreams. I hoped that, even briefly, the stillness of Auvillar quieted his demons.

In *place des halles*, Gerhard and I stood in the drizzle. Finally, Gerhard zipped his jacket. "He wanted to come back here and thank the villagers. They saved his children. He was grateful. I believe this."

I, too, believed that Sigismond Hirsch was grateful to the villagers. I also believed that his soul was restless and that conscious and unconscious forces drove him. He bought his houses, intending to form a community within a community, bringing city folks, rich folks, people "from away." They would come here on holiday. In my hometown on the coast of Maine, rich folks were building second homes and mansions while folks who had lived in town all their lives struggled to hold onto modest dwellings. These folks from away demanded services and, instead of lowering taxes, often raised them.

Sigismond Hirsch sought to make his claim in soil where the Gestapo had taken him and his wife. He was not a stupid man. He must have understood much faster than I that someone in Saint Michel, Auvillar, or another nearby village, had betrayed him. Had he wanted to walk among these villagers as a visible reminder of that treachery? Had he wanted the villagers to bear witness?

Perhaps, though, his motives were unselfish and altruistic, and he was thinking only of his saved children. Perhaps he'd truly wanted to create a utopian community — a bubble in time where he and his friends could live values embedded in Torah and perform *tzdekakah*, righteous acts that were a gift of the self. These were the values Mama had taught me when she would carry a jar of chicken soup to Mrs. Botkin who wasn't well, or when she offered lodging to a neighbor's son, a soldier returning from the war. Was the thought of altruism possible after Auschwitz? I liked to think Sigismond Hirsch returned to Auvillar to remember a brilliant October day when he, his wife, his son, and his friends walked in a garden, his baby daughter in his wife's arms. After this war, Sigismond Hirsch's nights were troubled. He was troubled.

"It was a shame," Gerhard said. "Hirsch only sold two of his houses."

In the early eighties, the mayor of Collonges-la-Rouges formed an association to save and preserve France's villages, envisioning tourism as their economic base. This was the beginning of France's *beaux villages*, and in order to become a *beau village*, a candidate village filled out an application. In Auvillar, the mayor and his council desperately wanted this designation, but how could Auvillar meet the association's criteria with Hirsch's houses decaying in the heart of the village?

What did Robert know? A few days later, we met on the terrace of Hotel de l'Horloge where a bartender set two cups of espresso on our table. Officially, this terrace was closed, but not for Robert. The owners were the first people in Auvillar who befriended him. Robert stirred sugar into his coffee and looked down into his cup. He'd lived in this village for twenty-five years, and it had taken him nearly that long to find friends. Like himself, his friends were French, but all were outsiders. When Robert arrived, Hirsch's houses were a blight, and they were dangerous, with roof tiles falling into the street, walls crumbling and jeopardizing adjacent buildings. Hirsch's name was synonymous with ruin, Robert said. "People were angry. They said he wouldn't fix his houses because they would not elect him mayor."

I set my espresso cup down in my saucer. I thought of the rumor about Robert's father retraining German police dogs after the war. That hadn't made sense, either. "Robert, why would a man living in Paris want to be mayor of Auvillar?"

Robert shrugged.

"Do you believe that?"

"I am telling you what people said."

Right. But I was growing frustrated. "Did anyone speak of Sigismond's torture at the hands of the Gestapo? Of Berthe's murder?"

"People spoke only of their parents' suffering. That they were poor. That they had nothing to eat."

"Auschwitz?"

"No one spoke of Auschwitz."

And so, Hirsch's story was truncated. Abbreviated. Whitewashed. In the eyes of the villagers, he was a Jew who'd come to Auvillar during the war and returned to Paris where he belonged. He bought houses. Then he let them crumble. No one liked him.

For days, I mulled over Robert's story. Did Hirsch really want to become mayor? Why wouldn't he sell? What of the village becoming a *beau village?*

I asked Gerhard. "For this we must talk to Odette," Gerhard said. "I will arrange this."

⌐

On another rainy day with Gerhard at my side, I rang Odette's bell. She ushered us into her parlor and seated us at a round table. Porcelain cats sat on shelves. Pictures of cats hung on walls. A cat lay curled on a love seat. Seconds passed before I realized the cat on the love seat was breathing. Speaking of Hirsch, Odette said, "He put up posters. Houses he wanted to sell. Then, when someone approached, he said, 'No, I have no houses to sell.'"

"Why? What was he doing?" I said.

She turned a slim gold wedding ring on her finger and I thought of Maurice, her husband, perhaps working with Hirsch during the war, the two men risking their lives to save others. I wondered whether Maurice had been one of the resistance fighters sitting at the kitchen table inside the grand château when the Gestapo burst in. I remembered a story Gerhard told as we drove back to Auvillar that afternoon. A neighbor living in the house across from the château, the same house where Gerhard had knocked to retrieve the absent key, used to watch Sigismond Hirsch pump water from the iron pump into a bucket, then empty the bucket onto his flowers. This neighbor did not have enough water for his family and he watched *le docteur* pour water into the dirt. Was Hirsch callous and insensitive? Had he understood his neighbor's plight? The neighbor would not have asked for water; he would have fumed and harbored deep resentment. That was the way here. Hirsch was urban; he was a Jew; he didn't belong. In wartime France, discontent often meant the difference between life and death. A slip of the tongue. A hint to a third party. An anonymous letter.

Odette was much younger than Maurice. She had not spent the war years in Auvillar. Her stories came from her husband, long since dead, who had told them to her after the war had ended. Perhaps her sympathy for Hirsch stemmed from her love of Maurice, or from her own relationship with Hirsch. Before assigning a task, Hirsch would ask her, "Do you have the time?" She liked that. Whatever the source, Odette held Sigismond Hirsch close to her heart. She stopped turning the gold ring. "I do not know what he was doing."

Odette rested her elbows on the table. "He said he would not take what they offered a beggar. It was good fair price. He would not accept it. People were angry."

Was Hirsch holding on to his dream? Or was he, as most villagers thought, punishing them and keeping the village from becoming a *beau village*?

"I think it was at the end when he became difficult," Gerhard said.

The doorbell rang and Odette left to answer. She led a large woman wearing a tan raincoat into the parlor. Gerhard shot me a look and I knew immediately that he did not like or trust this woman.

She pulled out a chair and sat erect at the table. Her presence sucked air from the room. I thought it odd that she hadn't removed her coat.

Reaching into a pocket, she pulled out a bottle and moved it across the table toward Odette.

"Truffle oil," Gerhard announced. "This is a delicacy."

Pleased, the woman nodded.

Gerhard introduced me as an American writer interested in learning about Sigismond Hirsch, and, without being asked, the woman — Madame somebody — launched into a story: "After the Yom Kippur War, Hirsch had the idea of starting a Jewish community here."

So, folks did think he wanted to bring a Jewish community to Auvillar. But the Yom Kippur War? She was way off. The Yom Kippur War, also known as the 1973 Arab-Israeli War, began when an Arab coalition launched a surprise attack on Israeli positions in the Israeli-occupied territories. Hirsch began buying his houses in 1951, more than twenty years earlier. I opened my mouth to correct her, but Gerhard shot me a look. I was grateful he'd curbed my impulse, for I'd taken my own measure of this woman, that she was unsettling, a troublemaker.

She puffed out her ample chest and said of Hirsch, "He walked around like this. Like De Gaulle."

Arrogant. Aristocratic.

Wasn't that Dreyfus's fatal flaw, his aristocratic bearing, his arrogance? A young captain in the French Army, Alfred Dreyfus was too French for a Jew. How could these army officers, these true Frenchmen, tell he wasn't one of them if he passed so easily? His commanders framed him and accused the young captain of giving secrets to the Germans. A closed-door court-martial convicted him. This was the old conundrum — get rid of your Jewish ways and assimilate, but not so much that we can't detect who you are, for if we can't tell the difference between you and us, how will we keep you out of our private clubs and our daughters' beds?

I thought of my father and his deep desire to assimilate. Had this been *his* wish or was he unconsciously responding to Christian demand?

I assumed this woman was anti-Semitic, but her bias could have been based on class or on Hirsch as an outsider. Or some blending of the three. She spoke of Jean Hirsch's book about his father, *Réveille-toi Papa, c'est fini!, (Wake up, Papa, It's Over)* a book in French that was not translated into English, a book I couldn't read, a book Gerhard had read.

"I think what his son says of him is not factual," the woman said. "I would say Jean Hirsch is not an historian."

Both Gerhard and Valerie had questioned Jean Hirsch's version of history, but neither had made me feel as if that questioning were tainted with doubt about the family's suffering. Or about the importance of the *Shoah* itself. I could see this woman as a Le Pen supporter. Quickly, Gerhard changed the subject. "Is it raining? I see you are wearing your raincoat. We need rain. Fall is here. Maybe now we will get rain."

Conversation turned to fields and crops, the fall harvests of grapes, apples, and mushrooms. Gerhard stood and we took our leave. Outside, the sky was the color of lead, and rain misted. The gray cobblestones were shining and slick. Gerhard lifted the collar of his jacket. "I did not want to engage. This woman stirs in the soup. Her husband is a town official."

Stirs in the soup. Stirs the pot. I realized Odette's visitor had no idea I was Jewish. Nor did Odette. The assumption was that I, like everyone else here, was Christian. Was I the child I used to be, still hiding my identity?

In the living room of the Maison Vielhescazes, a new heating unit was not working and a damp chill seeped through the old stone walls. I longed for a fire in the empty fireplace, but the chimney was not safe and fires were not allowed. I figured we were the ones who were unsafe, we artists and writers who could not be trusted with a fire. I was a New Englander, accustomed to building and watching a fire, its mesmerizing flames warming more than my chilled bones. I plugged an electric heater into the one outlet across the room. Heat did not reach the couch where I sat opposite Robert. It was a Sunday afternoon and I'd invited him for tea. I wrapped my shawl around my shoulders.

Robert looked down at his fingers as if surprised to see he'd been folding a candy wrapper into smaller and smaller squares. He set the wrapper on a low table between us. "I have a friend, a journalist. A week ago, maybe more now, his mother died," Robert said. "She lived in Valence d'Agen, and she was nearly a hundred and one. She was the widow of an important man, a very prominent politician. Because of this, a priest from Toulouse was summoned to say her Mass. People talked. Why is this woman so special? Why a priest from Toulouse? Why is the local priest not good enough? Maybe, she has no right to a Mass. You see, she was Jewish. She converted."

I sat back. *You see, she was Jewish. She converted.*

Another complex history that dropped me into yet deeper history. During the Inquisition, officials forced Jews to convert. Many did. Rumors started, neighbors saying that Jews were secretly practicing Jewish ritual. Most folks believed that a converted Jew was not and could never become a true Christian, an understanding deeply embedded in Christian lore. How the remnants of history surfaced like shards of glass slowly making their way from deep inner flesh to skin. The Inquisition, Vichy history — damned if you do, damned if you don't — damned in the Christian sense of the word, the Jew destined for hell.

Robert crossed a leg over one knee, making a figure four. "I wanted to know more, so I made an inquiry. Like you. When I took a coffee in Valence d'Agen, I asked people. 'What do you know of this woman?' They told me stories. She lived in Paris during the war. She had protection at the highest levels. This was how she survived." He uncrossed his legs and leaned across the table. "You know René Bousquet?"

Did I "know" René Bousquet? He was *only* Vichy's chief of police, a man notorious for his role in mass deportations, especially those of

Jewish children. At his trial in 1949, officials questioned Bousquet briefly and superficially. Judges gave him a nominal five-year sentence, a sentence magically lifted almost immediately. After his trial, he became an advisor and confidant of François Mitterrand. For decades, human rights leaders fought to bring Bousquet to justice. They finally succeeded in the early 90's but, on the eve of his trial in June 1993, an assassin posing as a delivery man shot Bousquet in the doorway of his flat. The only ones rejoicing were *Shoah* revisionists who had done everything in their power to slow justice because a Bousquet trial would have examined Vichy's record in the glare of the public eye.

I remembered visiting a young painter's studio in La Ruche on a visit to Paris. La Ruche was a beehive structure designed by Gustave Eiffel as a wine rotunda for the Great Exposition of 1900, later dismantled, then re-erected as working studios for artists. In its heyday La Ruche offered studio space to such greats as Chagall, Leger, Modigliani and Rivera. As I walked a path, I thought of their footsteps. This was not a place open to the public; I was with invited friends. I missed a step and, instead of entering gracefully, I stumbled into a room at ground level. This studio was a jumble of the resident artist's work — canvases resting on easels and leaning against walls, opened paint tubes, palettes with gobs of paint, and a jumble of his domesticity, clothing strewn on a narrow, unmade bed, dirty dishes and cups filling a tiny sink. Nearly every surface was covered. I didn't know where to rest my eyes.

I stood in front of a large black and white drawing propped on an easel. I couldn't take my eyes from the image — a concentration camp victim, emaciated. The artist's brush strokes stretched the figure's arms and bound his legs. This was Jesus on the cross. This was Auschwitz. My friends busied themselves with other images before leaving. Rooted to the horrifying beauty of this piece, I stayed. The artist, a young man maybe in his thirties, with disheveled black hair, stood off to one side, eyes cast downward. I approached him. "It's beautiful, but so sad. What drew you to this?"

In his broken and accented English, he said, "Because we don't know. In school, no one tells us."

So hard to believe, that in this, the twenty-first century, certain schools did not teach the *Shoah*. I thought of France's 1982 terrorist bombing of a Jewish delicatessen in the Marais that ushered in waves of attacks on Jews, on Jewish shops and schools, synagogues. Many of these attacks were met with government silence.

The artist shrugged. "I try to give away. No one wants."

I understood. I didn't want the drawing, either. Who could live with that image?

As I walked the quiet paths of La Ruche, the image trailed me like a shadow. So many ways to see the drawing: Christ as victim, victim as Christ, Christian as Jew, Jew as Christian. Jesus was a Jew and a reformer, but always a Jew. Jesus as Christ came later — much later, mostly a creation of Paul, originally Saul, a Jew. So, what did it mean to be a Jew?

Was Judaism a religious practice with adherence to certain rules? Were there such things as Jewish values? It seemed to me that values I might label as Jewish — devotion to family, giving to charity, caring for the sick, treasuring learning and education — were not exclusively Jewish; they also belonged to Christians, Muslims, Hindus, and all other faiths as well. And to those who professed no religion. I asked myself what made art, literature, or music Jewish? Must a Jew have created the work? What about non-Jews expressing Jewish themes? The young French artist was not a Jew. Was his work Jewish? Was it French? Was it an expression of our humanity, the horrors we perpetrated on one another and his plea for us to stop? To please stop now?

We cannot reverse history, but we can choose memory over forgetfulness.

Robert drank from his cup of tea. "Some people say my friend, the journalist, is not the son of the prominent politician, that he is the son of René Bousquet. This was his mother's lover. I do not know." Robert gazed into the space between us. "There are lots of stories like this in France. Here, people know the dust is still under the carpet."

PART III

16

Back in Paris for a week after my residency, I descended the winding staircase to the breakfast room in the basement of the Hotel Saint Paul le Marais, my pied-a-terre in Paris. At the entrance an iron gate sat open on its hinges. I entered beneath a stone arch. The walls were also stone, and I felt as if I were inside a wine cellar or a cave, perhaps a dungeon. The room was not unpleasant with its wooden tables, blue-and-yellow placemats, long table displaying an array of breakfast breads, cheeses, cereals, jams, and meats — but it was closed-in.

In an egg cooker, an electric appliance with a water bath, a timer, and indentations, I boiled my egg. At my table, I whacked off the top with the back edge of my knife just as Papa had taught me. Whack off the top and scoop egg up and out of the shell. I buttered a slice of dark bread and spread it with jam. In Mama's kitchen, I'd teethed on hard crusts of rye bread and pumpernickel.

Mama and Papa's roots were in Poland and Russia. Mama was thirteen, escorting her two younger brothers when their ship sailed into New York harbor. Both her parents had gone on ahead, and she was left to close up the family farm, so the story went. Teachers placed her in a classroom with six-year-olds. How was a girl who'd closed up a farm and crossed an ocean supposed to learn with six-year-olds? She left school and never learned to read or write in English, and all of her life her speech, whether English, Russian, Polish or Yiddish, sang with a Yiddish lilt. I didn't speak Yiddish, *Mama Loshen*, the mother tongue, but I understood the music of Mama's words, their intonation, their cadence, and I learned to make my voice sing that way. But not out loud. Not in front of my father.

German Jews did not speak Yiddish, and for my father this was a point of pride. He was not like those "other" Eastern European Jews. "No Yiddish. We speak English," he admonished Mama. On *Shabbos*, when my Uncle Irving tore a hunk of challah and passed it to my father, my father would pass the bread along without tasting. German Jews did not tear bread; German Jews sliced.

Germaine's family had roots in Spain, Italy, Greece, Austria, Egypt, and France. Probably my father's family had as many claims to countries as hers before settling in the Alsace-Lorraine, but they were unknown to me. Still, I understood that European culture had shaped me, giving me the fragrant smells of Mama's kitchen, the Yiddish lilt of her speech, and a closely bonded family. Sitting alone at my table in this windowless breakfast room, I felt something shifting inside me as if the proportions of my life were changing. In France, I'd found threads that linked me to my particular past and to the pasts of my people, Jews expelled from host country after host country, all searching and settling, never completely, because a diaspora population lived on the fringes. We carried our foods and our beliefs in invisible sacks on our backs, and those of us who thought we belonged often found ourselves talked about behind our backs. People whispered that we looked or didn't look Jewish. We were tight with a dollar or we were spendthrifts. Such were the extremes of stereotyping. No matter where we settled, we walked a narrow bridge. Commonality needed to learn to contain not only *our* difference, but all difference.

⤝

Over sparkling water and sweets — small apricot jellied tarts and frosted chocolate cookies — Yvonne, Valerie and I spoke of Yvonne's post-war life. At war's end Yvonne lived in a house run by the OSE, *Oeuvre des Secours Enfants*, the Children's Aid Society, in Limoges. Like the wartime Jewish Scouts, the OSE ran safe houses and saved Jewish children. Post-war, they housed and fed the survivors.

Yvonne was fifteen. Her parents had no money, no will, and no place to go. They traveled to Beaulieu sur Dordogne, the village of their survival and of their children's survival, where they rented a tiny basement flat and sustained themselves on government assistance. They neither could nor wanted to return to Germany. Ernst was not well; he needed an operation at a clinic in Tulle, about twenty-five miles north.

The name of the town must have haunted him. During the war, Tulle was a stronghold of Communist resistance. The day after D-day, the Resistance attacked the German garrison and killed, maimed, or imprisoned the German soldiers stationed there. A division of the SS on their way to Normandy changed course to Tulle but, by the time they arrived, all of the resistance fighters had melted into the woods. Only the town's citizens remained. The Germans hanged 99 men and deported another hundred to death camps from which they never returned. Germaine spoke of this as one of her worst memories. Surely, Yvonne and her family knew of this, too.

In Tulle, Yvonne saw her father through his operation and cared for him for seven weeks. On her return, still living in the house run by the OSE, she went to classes and learned to paint on porcelain, her tuition paid by the "Joint." Perfect, she thought. She loved to draw. She loved to paint. Bored, she found herself painting the same design over and

191

over. Her fingers ached. She wanted to quit, but she needed a skill. What else could she do to earn money for herself and her parents?

On her sixteenth birthday, her Aunt Marthe surprised her with a visit. Aunt Marthe wanted to reopen her shirt factory and, now that Maurice had died, she needed Yvonne. She offered room, board, and a small salary. Sitting at a table in her flat, Yvonne looked down at her manicured nails. She had lovely hands, lovely fingers, not a bulge of arthritis at the knuckles. "It wasn't much," Yvonne said, "but it was more than what I had."

Gone were her dreams of attending university and becoming a kindergarten teacher or a psychologist. Gone was the soil on which both sides of her family had lived for generations, their bones sunk deep into troubled earth. She'd lost her country and her language. Her family had scattered, her parents living in a dark flat in Beaulieu sur Dordogne, Marion living in Switzerland and refusing Yvonne's pleas to come to France and help with their parents. Years later, when Marion returned, she relied on Yvonne to find her a job and a flat. "I still prepare her taxes," Yvonne said.

In the shirt factory, Yvonne counted out piece work. She checked each garment for quality and she calculated payment. She had an affinity for numbers, so Aunt Marthe asked her to keep the books. She was becoming adept at business. "What about weekends?" I asked. "What did you do for fun?" Then, I wondered, was fun possible for a sixteen-year-old who had grown up inside this war?

"I liked classical music on the radio," Yvonne said. Sundays, she listened to — Tchaikovsky, Dvorak and Brahms. She drew in her sketchbook. She formed a Jewish scouting group for adolescent girls and took them on hikes in the countryside. She enjoyed her time with the young scouts, hiking and organizing dances. She lifted a frosted cookie from a plate and said to me, "I was a second Maki."

Germaine.

I probed, gently. "You went to dances?"

"No, I did not dance."

"But you went on dates, maybe for a walk or to a café?"

Yvonne brought her fingers to the large amber pendant at her neck. "If a young man asked me to accompany him to a café, I did not go. I thought he was inviting me because of my aunt's money."

Distrust, doubt, and fear, the residue of war invisible on her skin. How would she find her way back into life — not the life she'd imagined before leaving Ludwigshafen, that was gone, but into joy, laughter, and the frivolity of youth? Perhaps frivolity was gone for good, but not joy. Not laughter.

Yvonne set two photographs before me. In one she is about seven or eight, a child standing in the courtyard in Ludwigshafen where she used to play with Ursula, her German friend. The courtyard where, in her dream, she smashed her porcelain doll. In the photo she wears a short-sleeved smocked cotton dress with puffed sleeves and a Peter Pan collar, a straw hat with a ribbon tied under her chin. She poses near bushes and a small tree; and, in the manner of Shirley Temple, she tilts her head and looks coyly from under her hat. I remembered the marquee advertising a Shirley Temple movie that she'd passed with her mother, Yvonne asking. "Why, Mutter, why can't I go inside?"

In the photo, Yvonne bends the long stem of a trumpet flower and rests the bloom on her arm. This was life before expulsion, life before war had taught her to tamp down every pulsing part of herself.

In the second photograph she is a young woman living in Sarreguemines. Her hair is short and tightly curled and, although she smiles sweetly, her body carries an air of skepticism. At the table, Yvonne rested her fingers at the border of the portrait. Again I noticed her lovely fingers, her manicured nails. "In Sarreguemines I did not like the provincial boys. I was waiting for something serious. I wanted to feel something."

Robert Lieser, the man Yvonne married, had spent the war years hiding in an empty flat in Occupied Paris. He'd moved in after a Jewish family had been arrested. The sympathetic landlord was hiding two Jewish women in another "empty" flat. What was one more Jew? Ironically, this flat was a few buildings down the street from where we sat, Valerie, Yvonne, and I looking out on the tops of chestnut trees in the Parc des Buttes Chaumont across the road.

Robert's mother, the daughter of a French aristocrat, not Jewish, died young. His father, a German Jew, was hiding in the countryside. Mostly, Robert had grown up in Germany and he spoke perfect, unaccented German. Every morning for the five years of Occupation, he dressed in his green Austrian jacket and his Austrian hat. He pulled the sealing tape from his door, reaffixed the tape, and left the building. Shoulders squared, he walked two blocks to the Rothschild Hospital of Ophthalmology on a corner, the same hospital Valerie and I had passed as we walked from the Metro stop. The Germans, of course, had taken over. In the cafeteria Robert helped himself to a tray, chose his breakfast, and took a seat at a table among German doctors and German military officers. This was the one meal he ate, daily. A classic story of survival — unless or until something went wrong. Nothing went wrong. With a spark in her eye, Yvonne said, "This was the man I married."

In the immediate aftermath of the war, Robert Lieser became a salesman, selling shoes on the road and, as he traveled, he searched for missing relatives. That was how he learned of a cousin, Maurice, in Sarreguemines. He did not know that Maurice had been murdered in Auschwitz. In Sarreguemines he discovered Marthe and Yvonne. Again Yvonne's fingers moved to the pendant at her neck. "I found the feeling I was looking for when I met my husband."

Robert was family, cousin to the man who, along with Aunt Marthe, had taken Yvonne into their home all those years ago. Robert was also the handsome stranger come to town, but he wasn't a stranger, and so their meeting must have felt like destiny. He'd grown up in Yvonne's lost country. He spoke her lost language. He lived in Paris, the city of her dreams. Consciously or unconsciously, she must have remembered that day long ago when she'd begged Aunt Toni, "Why, why can't I go to Paris. Why only Marion?"

Because his two brothers had married women who were not Jews, Robert had taken a silent vow: he would marry a Jewish woman. He was in his mid-thirties and it was time. Yvonne was days away from her twenty-sixth birthday. She'd always thought she'd marry at twenty-five. The fates and the stars had aligned.

Yvonne brought a third photograph to the table. In this one she and Robert stand on a porch outside the house in Sarreguemines. Yvonne wears a sleeveless silk dress with a deep soft collar. A vase of tulips sits on a table behind her shoulder. Robert wears a suit, a white shirt, and a tie. He stands stiffly, his eyes and his smile holding back. Yvonne leans into his shoulder with her whole body. Her face is pure joy. Fingers curled into a fist, she holds his lapel as if to say, I will never let you go.

Robert died in 2011. Although this was a long marriage, Valerie had hinted on numerous occasions that they were not happy.

This portrait was their wedding picture, taken in 1952 after they'd married in a civil ceremony in Sarreguemines. Later they would marry in a religious service in Saarbrücken, Germany, the city of Robert's birth and his bar mitzvah. The synagogue was burned down on Kristallnacht and later rebuilt. Neither Yvonne nor Robert wanted to live in Germany, but they returned to their home country and to Robert's synagogue as if to sanctify ancestral memory. They settled in Paris, moving to this flat where we sat drinking tea and eating small cakes.

Later that day, I wandered the Marais — in Yiddish the *pletzl*, referred to as the Jewish Quarter. I thought of the folks who had lived here before the infamous roundups of the summer of 1942. At that time, the Marais was home to a thriving community of Eastern European Jews, who had fled Poland, Russia, Bulgaria, Lithuania and later Austria, Germany, Czechoslovakia, and Hungary. Most were observant, either Conservative or Orthodox, but their Orthodoxy was not the ultra-Orthodoxy of today — Jews easily identifiable by their dress, who isolate themselves from the stream of modern life, who send their children to Jewish schools and govern their separate Jewish communities according to repressive rules.

Ironically, in the 1930s as Hitler came to power, Jews living in western Europe and Jews living in the *shtetls* of Eastern Europe were on a path toward modernization and assimilation. Orthodoxy was disappearing. After the war, the trauma of the *Shoah* changed this course and ultra-Orthodox communities grew in size and power, both in France and in the United States. Today, the Marais was once again home to Jews, most of them ultra-Orthodox, but they were not from Eastern Europe; they were Sephardic, who had emigrated mostly from Tunisia and Morocco.

In the 1800s when Baron Haussmann created his wide sweeping boulevards across Paris, the Marais escaped his demolition and renovation plans and retained its narrow cobblestoned streets and tiny lanes, teeming now with pedestrians — smartly dressed women walking in pairs or alone, some pushing strollers, others carrying briefcases, men wearing suits, teens in jeans and T-shirts, their leather jackets unzipped.

Rue de rossier was mostly a pedestrian walkway with an occasional motor scooter. Bicyclists wove among the crowd. I walked slowly, absorbing sights and sounds, storefronts painted bright yellow, emerald green or Persian blue. I listened to bicycle bells and the rapid-fire sounds of French. I breathed the sweet scents of butter and yeast wafting from Sasha Finkelstajn, a bakery displaying what Mama used to call *aeyer kikhl*, air cookies because they were crispy, crunchy, and light as air. I waited in a long line, then pointed. A woman behind a counter plucked three, then four. *"C'est bon,"* I said.

Outside the bakery and across the way, restaurant tables tilted on worn cobblestones. People talked, ate, and sipped from glasses of beer or wine. No matter the time of day in Paris, people ate. Waiters set down platters with smoked salmon and fragrant cheeses, baskets filled with slices of baguette, plates with *pommes frites*. I stood in front of Panzer, a delicatessen with a Star of David, its date written according to the Hebrew calendar: Since 5755, ie. 1994. Inside the shop, tubes of salami and bologna hung from hooks. Cases displayed hunks of brisket and whole tongues. These were the foods of my childhood: slices of salami, brisket, and tongue. Mama would boil a whole tongue in a pot on the stove, and I would watch the peppercorns and pickling spices swirl.

Again, I imagined life here before July 1942: women leaning out of third-story windows and shouting to the children below who were kicking balls in the street and jumping rope, men walking to prayer — a bustle of urban Jewish life. All would have been wearing a yellow cloth Star of David when the Germans, along with French police, emptied the Marais, herding men, women and children, even infants, into waiting buses, their destination the Vel d'hiv. Inside that airless building — with windows sealed shut, a glass roof painted black where daytime temperatures soared and nighttime temperatures plummeted — French police guarded more than thirteen thousand Jews, four thousand of them children. They had no food, no water, no toilets. Women gave birth. People grew sick. After five days, French police transported these wretched people to the intermediate detainment camp, Drancy, prior to sending them to Auschwitz.

I remembered the day I visited the memorial to the Vel d'hiv on Boulevard de Grenelle. As I stood off to one side, a woman wearing faded jeans and a bold red and black striped shirt approached. She was flanked by two girls who looked about twelve or thirteen. The girls, too, wore jeans, along with sleeveless shirts and sneakers, one pair white, the other pink. All three held tea candles. The woman lit a match, and they placed their burning candles on a cement curb just inside the iron fence. Assuming they spoke English, I approached. "That was so thoughtful. To bring candles," I said.

She motioned to the girls. "They read the book, *Sarah*... She searched for the title. "Ah *Sarah's Key*," I said.

In the popular novel, Tatiana de Rosnay fictionalizes the Paris round-ups and the imprisonment of Jewish families in the Vel d'hiv. I didn't read the book, but I saw the movie because I was looking for images for my research, but I found it unrealistic and sensationalist. Yet, *Sarah's Key* brought these girls to this history and to this place, and for that I am grateful. Deeply moved, the girls stood back and watched their candles glow.

I made my way to *rue des Hospitalières Saint Gervais* and stopped outside a stone courtyard. A gray iron fence protected both courtyard and building. Even from this distance I was able to read the carved stone plaque:

260 enfants Juifs de cette école
deportes en Allemagne durant
la seconde guerre mondiale
furent extermines
dans les camps Nazis

> *N'oubliez pas*

Loosely translated the plaque read: The Germans deported 260 Jewish children from this school during the Second World War for extermination in the Nazi camps. Do not forget.

Another day, walking along the Seine in the Fifteenth Arrondissement, I spotted a flight of stairs with a sculpture at the top. I found myself in an elevated park with grass, a walkway, and a sign that read Quai de Grenelle. An iron railing ran along the edge of the park and guarded a drop down to the river. Bolted to cement blocks, iron lampposts marched single file to the base of the Eiffel Tower in the distance. The park was quiet, an oasis above the street noise.

I stared at human shapes cast in bronze, a family, their bodies curving with sadness and compassion for each other, their gazes distant, as if each were trying to understand this terrible turn their lives had taken. They leaned toward one another, a mother cradling a small boy, a husband touching his wife's shoulder and, at their feet, their daughter holding a sleeping baby in her lap, one hand resting on the baby's cheek, the other on the baby's leg. The girl looked inward with knowledge beyond her years. The child in his mother's arms seemed to have exhausted himself with crying. A couple clung to one another, he holding her, she holding her pregnant belly. A single woman lay on her side, one arm bent and holding her head, the other arm resting on a valise. I translated the inscription at the sculpture's base. "In tribute to the victims of racist persecutions and crimes against humanity. Never forget."

This was a second memorial to the victims of the Vel d'hiv, their humanity cast in bronze. It was here in 1995 during a ceremony held two months after he had taken office that President Jacques Chirac publicly recognized France's responsibility for sending thousands of Jews to Nazi death camps, thus ending years of government equivocation.

17

Aline, the child who used to ride in the back basket of Germaine's bicycle in those post-war days, stood on the landing in front of her mother's flat. At seventy, she was stunning, with vibrant eyes and curly red-brown hair. Because she'd worked as a flight attendant for Air France and had lived in Michigan during an early marriage, Aline spoke fluent English. She lived in a flat downstairs that mirrored Germaine's in layout and décor, both choosing the same French provincial chairs — Germaine's upholstered in apricot velvet, Aline's in beige silk. "I didn't realize when I bought them," Aline said.

Valerie and I had each carried shopping bags with sandwiches and a bottle of wine, and I held a bouquet of roses, Germaine's favorite flower. Aline reached for my shopping bag. "I have a surprise for you," she said, giving me a wink. "Daniel is here. He's visiting from Belgium."

Daniel, the only one of Germaine's and Ralph's three children old enough to remember life in Beaulieu sur Dordogne and in post-war Paris. "Here? Now?" I exclaimed.

Aline peered into the shopping bag. "Truthfully, I am surprised he has agreed to speak with you. Generally, he does not speak on this subject."

Germaine accepted the roses and inhaled their sweet scent. She turned to her daughter. "Because of me."

Again, Aline winked. "Always because of you."

"Yes, because of me. I told him he must speak with Sandell."

In the kitchen, I ran water into a vase and carried it into the living room. Germaine put the roses down inside and fanned them into a spray of color — rose, peach, and the palest pink. She stepped back and rested her hand on her heart. "Oh, *les roses*."

The phone rang and Germaine hurried to answer. Aline filled me in on Daniel's visit: He and his wife were moving to the south of France, and Daniel was scouting out real estate. "In Belgium, the taxes are too high," Aline said.

Valerie countered. "In France the taxes are too high."

Taxes were the reason Valerie and Thierry were buying a flat in Switzerland. They hoped to move in the near future but moving to Switzerland was difficult. Many laws. Aline shrugged as if to say that was the way things went — everywhere the taxes were too high. Everywhere there were too many laws.

In an adjacent room, Germaine's voice rose and fell in rapid French. Satisfied her mother could not hear, Aline said, "Daniel has married three times. He has an older son with his first wife, a Corsican woman. With his second wife, he has no children. He married his third wife in 1990 and they have three daughters, all students. One plays the mandolin with an orchestra. The others are studying in Strasbourg. He is waiting downstairs in my flat. He did not want to interrupt our lunch. He will join us later for dessert."

I wanted to protest. *Interrupt our lunch? He would be the guest of honor.* I said nothing and took my place at the table.

That year, the French novelist Patrick Modiano had won the Nobel prize for literature and his photograph was posted everywhere — utility poles, fences, the sides of buildings, and walls inside the Metro. Modiano, born in 1945, wrote of German Occupation and French Collaboration, two poisons Parisians still breathed in the air.

"He is like me," Germaine said.

Aline lowered her wine glass. "What do you mean he is like you?"

Taking a hearty bite of her sandwich, Germaine spoke around the food in her mouth. "My family is like his family."

"Sephardic?", asked Aline.

Aline meant Sephardic in the old way of Jews leaving Spain and Portugal during the Inquisition, traveling across Europe to Turkey, a country that had welcomed them but not bestowed citizenship. This was Nissim Rousso's history.

"I mean my father is like his father," Germaine said.

Aline whispered, "Normally, she does not speak about this."

During the war Alberto Modiano, Patrick's father, was a collaborator, working with the Gestapo and trading on the black market. Albert Modiano spoke French and Italian, and probably German. Nissim Rousso, too, was a linguist, a man who spoke ten languages and was fluent in German. Neither Alberto Modiano nor Nissim Rousso had registered for the Jewish census and, although during Occupation this had protected them from deportation, it also prevented them from finding legal work, something I had only learned recently.

Germaine leaned an elbow on the table. "Now that I am old, I think about my father and what he did during the war. I do not know for certain. I am not sure. In war crimes there is the gray area. You know the gray area? Primo Levi speaks about this."

Primo Levi wrote several books recounting his experiences, among them, *If This Is a Man, Survival at Auschwitz,* and *The Drowned and the Saved.* The camp was not one camp but three, all using forced labor, one becoming a death camp as well as a labor camp. Levi squared up to the unspeakable evil inside Auschwitz and stated that everyone, the tortured and the torturers, were corrupted. The gray area was and is the zone where war and morality collide, a place where a person could not — without the experience of having been there — judge the actions of another. In Primo Levi's gray zone, the lines between good and evil are blurred.

Aline lifted her fingers to her cheek and rested them there. "She has told me this only recently. About my grandfather trading on the black market."

The windows were open and the whine of a car on a distant street was the only sound in the room. Wordlessly I lowered my sandwich to my plate. Valerie broke our silence. "Modiano writes about the Star. You know, the yellow star Jews wore during Occupation. He makes a joke in his novel. A Nazi soldier asks a man, 'Where is *la Place de l'Étoile?*' This is a very famous place in Paris, the Plaza of the Star, but the man who is Jewish does not give directions. Instead, he points to his jacket and the yellow Mogen David. He says to the soldier, 'Right here.'"

Mogen David. Star of David.

Aline remembered a day when she was a child, maybe eight. She was alone in the flat in the Thirteenth Arrondissment, though perhaps Léon was in his bedroom resting. She wandered into Léon's study. "I saw his papers and his books. One book was open to a page with people who looked like skeletons. I saw piles of dead bodies. I looked. I did not ask. Even when I saw those pictures, even when I heard Léon speak with his friends, all of them all the time talking religion, talking philosophy, culture and psychology, I did not link myself to this subject or to those people in the book. I did not think I was Jewish. I did not know what Jewish was."

I remembered when I had first seen those images. I, too, had been wandering the house. Alone in the living room, I leafed through pages

203

in *Life* magazine, but I identified so strongly with those dead bodies that I wanted to deny connection. Even before the war, there was an anti-Semitic stereotype of Jews as passive and weak. After the war, the stereotype took on the image that had haunted me: Jews led to the slaughter like sheep. Now, thinking back, I can understand why Germaine did not want to tell the children they were Jewish.

Aline was fifteen, a student in the *lycée*, when she learned that her last name, Weyl, was a Jewish name. "I don't remember who told me this. Someone in school. But it was the name. That is how I learned."

Yet, I suspected this knowledge of a Jewish connection had been there all along, folded into the deepest recesses of her subconscious.

Germaine drew herself up, her voice defensive. "It did not seem important to tell them."

Important. I ran the word through synonyms in my head: necessary, crucial, imperative, essential, significant.

When she was in her mid-twenties — a tall young woman with honey-colored hair and bright, energetic, intelligent eyes — Aline met Sydney, a Tunisian Jew. During the Second World War, Tunisia was the only Arab country to fall under direct German occupation. The government implemented a system of collaboration to enforce Nazi policies against Jews. Sydney was born there on November 1, 1943, after Allied troops had entered Tunisia, and that was why he bore an Anglo-Saxon name. When Sydney was eighteen, his family sent him to France to study for his baccalaureate and, shortly after that, his mother, his father, and his two younger sisters emigrated. The family celebrated all the Jewish holidays at home with prayers and ritual meals. They were visibly Jewish, and Sydney wore a big gold Jewish star on a chain around his neck. "I liked that," Aline said. "He was not afraid to say he was a Jew."

When I was a young child, I wore a tiny gold Jewish star, a gift from Mama. You needed to look closely to see that the pendant was a six-pointed star. The size of it pleased my father, and my near-visibility as a Jew pleased Mama. When I was eight, I stopped wearing the necklace. I agreed with my father, "Why advertise?"

Valerie spoke of two attitudes common among French Jews, those who didn't say they were Jewish, and those who were mostly of North African descent and wore the large Mogen David. "They have a right to be proud," Valerie said, "but I don't like the way they show off. There is something aggressive about their behavior."

They were not acting French. The way of French Jews was to assimilate. Many converted to Catholicism. "For generations families mixed," Valerie said. What she meant was that within families some were Jewish; some were Catholic. Cousins took Communion or became a bar mitzvah.

Aline and Sydney married under a *huppah*, the traditional Jewish wedding canopy, and Aline walked in ritual circles around the groom, protecting him from evil spirits and worldly temptations or, in a modern interpretation, defining the space of their new home. "Then, then is when I felt Jewish," Aline said. She reached and picked up her cell phone. "I will call Danny now."

Daniel wore jeans, a navy-blue pullover sweater with two gray stripes at the chest and three buttons, and a collar that was askew. He was nearly bald and so handsome with his crystalline blue eyes that I immediately remembered a story Germaine had told. One day in Beaulieu sur Dordogne when Daniel was three, two Nazi soldiers approached on the sidewalk. Germaine held tight to Daniel's hand and, as the soldiers passed, she overheard one say to the other, "Oh, they make such beautiful little Aryans here in France."

I remembered an archival photograph of another boy about three. This boy had dark sad eyes. He raised his hands in surrender. Pinned to the lapel of his tiny jacket, a yellow cloth Star of David and, in my imagination, I saw them side by side — the supposed Aryan child and the unnamed Jewish child. One would live; one would die.

I extended my hand. "*Enchantée.*"

Daniel smiled. "Pleased to meet you."

Like his sister, Daniel spoke fluent English. I was surprised. I don't know why. Germaine understood English and read books in English, such as E. M. Forster's *A Room with A View*, which she had shown me earlier, pointing out the English text. Probably, if she chose, she could join our conversation. I assumed she was too proud.

Her signature apple tart sat on the table, and as Aline set a knife gently into it, she looked at Daniel. It seemed to me that his expression hadn't changed, but Aline moved the knife and cut a larger wedge. Daniel smiled. I enjoyed watching this dance of gestures and looks, love expressed without words.

On the narrow balcony, mandevilla grew in pots and in window boxes, beautiful deep pink flowers that bloomed on vines and climbed trellises, a change from Germaine's usual geranium. Daniel peeled his sweater and carefully draped it over his chair, smoothing the wool and arranging the sleeves. He appeared calm; yet, I wondered if his careful, deliberate motions camouflaged agitation. Earlier, without specifying, Aline had alluded to "certain difficulties." I reminded myself that Daniel had been and, in a sense, still was a child of war, a child who at seven had chosen to leave his mother and live with his father and stepmother. He'd married three times, perhaps, I assumed, harboring deep conflicts within.

Aline filled him in on our conversation, saying we were speaking of Modiano, the Yellow Star, and pondering the meaning of being a Jew. Daniel said, "I had no sense of being Jewish."

I noted his use of the past tense, and I thought of my own perception of being Jewish, of feeling Jewish, and I realized that my notion of Jewish identity came, not only from living inside the yellow stucco house with Mama and Papa, but from my extended family. When you grew up with your Aunt Adele and your Uncle Irving dancing the rumba and the cha-cha-cha in the living room, with your Aunt Helen performing tricks with her three dogs, your Uncle Herman dancing the *kotche* at bar mitzvahs and weddings, Uncle Nat smoking his fat cigar and blowing smoke rings for your index finger, your father dropping nickels from your nose, your Aunt Ida singing *Bai Mer Bist Du Schön* as if she were one of the Andrews Sisters, and nearly all of your relatives telling their stories loudly enough to be heard outside of walls, cracking jokes and gesturing broadly, the whole lot of them overheated with boundless joy or bitter anger … well, then you felt like a Jew.

The Alsace region where Daniel had grown up was and is still notoriously anti-Semitic, and Ralph, his father, had kept his Jewish identity hidden. Daniel described this behavior as a "complete blackout." How strange for a man who'd worked with the Jewish Scouts and fought with the Resistance. On second thought, not so strange, for after the war many — both gentiles and Jews — blamed the Jews for their troubles, the Jews internalizing the anti-Semitism directed against them and buying into the simplification that they had been weak and walked like sheep to their slaughter, a simplification I had embraced. Daniel spoke of going to church with his Protestant stepmother and visiting her anti-Semitic family. "I heard anti-Semitic remarks but did not feel those remarks were directed at me," he said.

Was this denial or innocence? Inside the house where he grew up with his father and his stepmother, phantoms must have shadowed movement and speech. A child senses the unspoken. Daniel seemed to corroborate this. "I knew in some way I was Jewish. But I was not. I was double."

W. E. B. Du Bois, the African-American writer of the Harlem Renaissance, in his essays about race, coined the phrase *double consciousness*. "It is a peculiar sensation, this double-consciousness, this sense of always looking at one's self through the eyes of others, of measuring one's soul by the tape of a world that looks on in amused contempt and pity."

I knew this feeling of watching and I succumbed to self-censoring, of being raised to disappear inside a larger culture. In high school and college I would question myself: Was my voice too loud? Was I speaking with my hands? How was I supposed to hold this stupid teacup, gloves on or off? This would have been at Wilson College where I was required to attend afternoon teas in order to learn propriety and good taste. I was also required to attend daily morning chapel and one church service a month. Wilson was a Protestant-affiliated school. I sat dutifully and quietly through Christian service after Christian service, the juices in my belly curdling at the words: "In the name of our Lord, Jesus Christ."

Daniel said, "What is important to me concerning religion is that I don't want to belong to any organized dogma. I want to be able to live anywhere. I don't like particularism, I like universality. I like oneness. This is the part of me that is Jewish."

His association of oneness with his Jewish side interested me, for this was what could save us all, an understanding that inside of difference we were one, Christian, Jew, Muslim, Buddhist, Hindu, any religion we named, all bound by our common humanity. I understood. I wanted to claim my Jewish identity in my own way, choosing my rituals, praying or not praying. But to many Jews and, especially to Orthodox and ultra-Orthodox Jews, I was not a Jew.

Most of all I didn't want others to link me to Israeli politics or to the extreme beliefs of the ultra-Orthodox, religious or political. Like Daniel, I didn't want anyone telling me what I could or could not believe, what I could or could not eat, whom I could or could not love. One time Germaine asked me what I liked about being Jewish, and I answered, "The stories. I love the stories."

For me the Hebrew Bible is an intergenerational novel, an intriguing document of character, narrative, and psychology, an affirmation of the complexity of our lives. The text is open and alive with possibility, lending itself to dialogue and interpretation. Rabbis have argued with that text for centuries. It was no accident that Jews breaking into the world of academe and obtaining professorships in American universities in the late '40s and early '50s — men, of course — chose literature as their field. They were — we are — people of the book and, in my opinion, this does not mean letter of the law; this means *midrash*, story.

My sister-in-law, raised Jewish but nonpracticing, married a Protestant man, and they joined the UU Church, Unitarian Universalist, a church that welcomes all religions. They raised their three children in this church. For me, the UU Church is like a chocolate bar melting on a hot summer day, gooey, sticky, and running thin. I needed Mama's Yiddish melodies playing in my ear. I needed her hands circling the *Shabbos* flames. I needed her gaze lifted to the ceiling as she railed against God. "*Nu*, God, I'm such a bad person, you should give me such *tsurus*?"

Trouble.

I recalled girls, flanked by a statue of the Virgin and Child and the open door of the massive Abbey of Saint Peter in Beaulieu sur Dordogne, linking hands and forming a Star of David as they sang *Ma Tovu*, Germaine giving the downbeat. I needed that crazy juxtaposition, that crazy complexity.

Daniel said, "Many people in the Alsace regret that Hitler lost the war. They say that with Hitler there was order."

This was not the first time I'd heard this sentiment expressed. In Auvillar when Robert had spoken to me of his mother, a conservative and traditional Catholic, he said she too had expressed a desire for Nazi order and the unspoken Christian whiteness of her known world. Traditionally, Jews in Europe were, like America's blacks at the time, taking the rap for whatever went wrong.

"Now in the Alsace they also hate Arabs," Daniel said.

Germaine reached under her glasses and rubbed her eyes. "I have a friend. We went to a concert. She does not know I am Jewish."

Aline interrupted. "I think she knows you are Jewish."

Germaine fixed her gaze on her daughter. "She does not know."

Aline winked.

Germaine turned away from her daughter. "My friend points to the name of the conductor on the program. She said to me, 'This conductor, he is Jewish.' She would not say, 'He is Catholic.'"

"But she could have said he is black or Chinese,'" Aline countered. "That's the racism in France, black, Chinese, Arab, Jew. They say Chinese because they don't know anything else. For them all Asians are Chinese."

I probed, saying to Germaine. "Did you tell her? Did you say 'I am Jewish?'"

Answering for her mother, Aline said, "You cannot do that here."

I wanted my French friends to acknowledge their heritage and history. But, what was I thinking? They were holding a mirror to my face. This was what I wanted to do, stand tall and say to the world, I am a Jew. No more childish games. No more now you see me, now you don't. No more being a Jew only inside the comfortable world of other Jews. American culture assumed a certain level of well-being for the "socially Christian," deciding which holidays were important and merited celebration. In my hometown, where my granddaughter went to high school, teachers scheduled tests on Yom Kippur, and the director of the honors choir expected his few Jewish students to sing Christ's praises every year in a holiday concert without a nod to other religions around the world. This was not okay.

❧

I'd married the most un-Jewish Jew I could find. Dick was four years older than I and working as a salesman in Cincinnati for a New England firm, Gorton's of Gloucester. Growing up, he and his family had had a Christmas tree. They had never celebrated *Shabbos* or *Pesach*. Not even a pair of brass candlesticks sitting on a bookshelf or a mantel.

Dick had embraced assimilation. At that time, I had too. He walked tall in the world and I wanted to walk tall beside him. He courted me with tickets to the symphony, dates at a jazz club, dinner at a French restaurant where a waiter served me *poisson en papillote*, a preparation that both delighted and startled. After we married I took his name, Morse, an Anglo name, changed from Maas to Morse shortly after his ancestors had arrived on these shores. I thought I would have it all — sophistication, marriage, children, and the mostly Christian intellectual path I'd begun in college.

I remembered a night long ago. I walked from the den to an open doorway. In the living room, the lights of my Christmas tree blinked. For me the tree did not have religious significance. That's what I told myself. A lie. The tree is a Christian symbol. In the sixteenth century, devout Christians in Germany started the tradition when they brought trees into their homes and decorated them for Christmas.

Outside, the headlights of a car passing on the road streaked the walls. The stairs creaked. Wearing his footie pajamas, Richard, my oldest son, descended. At my side, the dog wagged her tail. I lifted my hand to the top of Richard's head and rested my palm lightly. "What are you doing up?"

"Couldn't sleep."

I moved my hand to his shoulder and drew him close. "Bad dream?"

He shook his head.

"Then what?"

"Don't know."

The lights on the tree sparkled. "Pretty, isn't it?" I said.

"Mom, can we just light a menorah?"

"We do," I said.

"Just a menorah."

"You mean no tree?"

He reached for the dog and nodded. "It's too confusing."

A spirited exchange erupted at the table. Earlier we'd talked of Germaine's bicycle, the one she rode through post-war Paris pedaling the children to school. Germaine remembered two baskets, one draped over the handle bars and one attached to the back fender. "No," Daniel said, "only one basket on the front for Arlette."

"Yes, of course there was a basket for Aline," Germaine said.

"No basket," Daniel said. "Aline rode on the seat."

"And you?" Germaine asked.

"I rode on the back."

Daniel recalled the steep hill and his mother speeding down without brakes. He touched his index finger to his temple. "She was crazy."

We all laughed because we loved Germaine's craziness. We loved Germaine and this was what united us all, love crossing cultures and crossing a sea. As for that second basket, I believed Daniel, and it was as if I were seeing them all — Daniel, Aline, Arlette, and Germaine — holding tight and speeding into their day.

We need many voices to tell our stories, for the truth lies not in each voice, but in the context of our blended notes. I, too, the storyteller, imagined my version of Germaine on her bicycle, placing her in the warmth of a spring day, pedaling the rutted streets and dodging piles of rubble. Somewhere in the midst of our different stories, we find our common humanity.

18

I first met Odile, a French artist, when we were both Fellows in residence at the Virginia Center for the Creative Arts in Amherst, Virginia, and although we barely spoke one another's language, something inexplicable sparked a connection. We weren't close in age, but both of us were mature enough to have had similar experiences with adult children and long marriages. When I visited with Odile in Montauban, I climbed into her silver Mercedes van, a vehicle large enough to transport her art, as she often worked on large canvases.

In Virginia, at open studios, when artists invited other Fellows to view their work, we would stand side by side, each holding a glass of wine, nodding and admiring an artist's use of color and light or perhaps her unique incorporation of words onto her canvas. One evening, before reading from an essay I'd written about Germaine, I gave her a hard copy of the piece. The next day, as we sat in a gazebo and gazed out at the wide expanse of lush Virginia lawn, Odile talked about Vichy France. Her great-grandparents had lived in Lourdes, a town near the Spanish border, and during the war they ran an inn there. Devoutly Catholic, they were part of a network of priests, nuns and monks, all working to save resisters and Jews. "My mother told me she saw people staying at the inn for only a night before moving on, probably to the border with Spain," Odile said.

Today the back of Odile's van was empty. It was November, cool and breezy. After leaving Paris, I'd gone to Auvillar, then come by train, about an hour's ride. Odile and I drove into the countryside, our destination Septfonds, the internment camp where the families deported from Auvillar had been imprisoned — Bruno, Gisèle, and Adèle Kurzweil; Regina and Manfred Moriz; Liselotte and Bernard Roth; Sigismond and Anna Winewiez; Ernst Weisselberg and his son. I knew I would not see an actual camp. That was long gone, but the site remained. Odile used to drive to Septfonds, a village with the same name, every day. She'd rented a studio there and the odd thing was that before I spoke with her about the camp, she hadn't known of its existence.

Built in January 1939 to house the multitudes of Spanish Republican refugees fleeing Spain, the camp later housed foreign workers and other refugees. Conditions were foul, no running water, no heat, no electricity. The camp closed briefly in 1941, then reopened in 1942 as part of Hitler's Final Solution when it was transformed into a holding camp for Jews rounded up in that infamous year.

I looked for road signs. I read my map. "I think we need to turn soon," I said.

She slowed the car. "Here?"

The two-lane road was lined with forests. My map showed a single road entering from the left. "This has to be it."

This road was narrower than the first and, like most country roads, the sides fell away into deep ditches. Ours was the only car traveling in either direction. I saw no houses, no long drives, no cultivated fields. A stone church with blue shutters and a red-tiled roof sat on a knoll. Beside the church, a large wooden cross held a life-like figure of Jesus.

Nothing figurative about that rendering. People must be living nearby, I thought.

Just past the church, a dirt drive led to our destination. I wasn't sure how we knew to turn, but both of us nodded at once. Odile parked. Barbed wire enclosed a large expanse of barren land. I looked for a guard or for a volunteer, someone to guide us. No one. We sat in the car without speaking, each of us understanding that when we stepped out and touched earth, history would seep through the soles of our shoes and into our flesh. No turning back. Finally, Odile sighed. "Ready?"

Beyond the barbed wire, hills undulated beyond the large grassy plain. Odile and I stood at the fence where hundreds and thousands of hungry, tired, cold, frightened people had stood looking out, all waiting for their unnamed cruel destiny. I felt their eyes and averted my gaze. A sparrow alighted on a spindly bush and rocked on a branch. The silence was deep, and time paused as if caught inside a single breath.

Odile walked to a wooden building that resembled a shack. It was the one remaining barracks and had a large fading, black number "34" under the pitch of the roof.

Inside, the space was bare. A drawing tacked to a wall showed what the place had looked like with three hundred and fifty cots lined up. The picture did not show the people, but prisoners had lain on those cots side by side, inches separating one from the next.

Odile tugged at her jacket and then, making a fist, held it closed. Distress washed over her face. We walked from the barracks to a three-sided shed. This, apparently, was the information center. Plastic sleeves held typewritten pages with lists of names and copies of photographs, all tacked to wooden boards. Inside the plastic, the paper had curled and yellowed; writing had faded. A breeze blew into the shed and ruffled the sleeves. How long before a final windstorm carried these sheets into ditches and fields? Perhaps these were replacements of others. But if no one came here — and it appeared as if few, if any, came — how would anyone know these papers and these names had gone missing?

I searched until I found her, Adèle Kurzweil, 17. "This is her," I said to Odile, "the girl I was telling you about."

Odile wiped tears.

Listed on the same paper was Frédérique Hirsch, 13. Again that name — my name. Any relation to Sigismond and Berthe? Recently, Yvonne had told me that she had Hirsch relatives. Her great-grandfather was a Hirsch. Two cousins of her father were named Hirsch, one went to England, the other to Stockholm. All were from the Alsace-Lorraine. I found Sigismond and Berthe's names and felt a shared heritage binding us all. The youngest children on the list were three years old: Edith Englehart and Dora Jesionwiez.

An odd quietness came over us. I felt empty yet solid at the same time, ethereal yet made of stone. Why and how had this genocide happened? There was no logic, nothing to grab hold of. Ideology was abstract; human suffering was not. Yet, we continue to inflict horrors on one another, closing borders, building refugee camps, building walls and giving power to ideologues who feed on our fears and vulnerability. But for an accident of birth, each of us could have been the other, born elsewhere, living elsewhere. None of us is entitled to a damn thing; yet, none of us deserves this.

We stood in that shed for a long time, each sensing and waiting for the other. Finally, I took a breath signaling I was ready.

Outside, I photographed a marble monument with an inscription that remembered the Jews of Septfonds, 1939 to 1944. The monument itself dated from 1996, and it struck me, as it usually did, how long it had taken folks to remember. From the looks of things, not many were remembering this site, now. No markers on the road. Weathered and faded documentation. A feeling of abandonment and neglect.

Odile led me across the road. She'd been studying the layout of the camp, and now she was showing me an outdoor laundry where prisoners used to wash their clothes. I wasn't sure how it all worked — a shallow stream, a water pump, a cement holding tank. "They would kneel at the stream," Odile said.

Men, women and children scrubbing cloth against rock, an ordinary task to let each person know that here, on the brink of mortality, he or she was alive.

"So hard to believe," Odile whispered.

And that was the crux, wasn't it? So hard to believe that many chose not to, and this was what the Nazis had counted on, our disbelief and our willingness, if not to say that it never happened, then to put it aside. And we did that in so many ways, friends saying to me: *I'm finished reading about the Holocaust. No more books about World War Two. Done. It's over.* My own censor chiming in and silently whispering in my ear. *What do you think you're doing writing about Vichy France? How can you possibly add to the existing mountain of material on this subject? You're not an historian. You're not a journalist. You're not even French. What chutzpah.*

The sun dropped and the air cooled quickly. Wind rattled yellow beech leaves clinging to branches. Still, we lingered. As we walked the dirt track back to Odile's van, I checked my watch. Nearly an hour and a half had passed without my awareness. I wondered when another person would stop here, walk here, think here.

As if to bring the past to the present, Odile drove through the village of Septfonds, passing a *boulangerie*, a *tabac*, a *pharmacie*, a pizzeria, a post office, a café, and a market that opened only on Wednesday mornings. Odile pointed out the building where she used to rent a studio. She showed me the house of the German commandant. She, too, had done her research. "When I knew you were coming here, I asked around," she said. The massive stone structure must have been grand, but now it looked only large. There were no bushes, trees, or gardens, only this dirt parking lot. The house had been divided into apartments, and as we left, I counted nine mailboxes — time layering over history.

⁂

The next day, I found an empty table outside a restaurant at Place Nationale, a central square surrounded by buildings constructed of Montauban's classic red brick. Waiters set down plates with grilled fish, salads with shrimp or squid, plates with *magret de canard*, filet of duck. Under a colonnade that surrounded the plaza, restaurants and shops abounded — patisseries; boulangeries; cheese artisans; a corner market displaying prunes, assorted nuts, apples, pears, oranges, grapefruit, plums, and grapes; all the shops now opening after the mid-day close. My mind lingered in past time, Vichy France, Adèle and Septfonds. All of this plenty was a strange juxtaposition. I felt uneasy. I was hungry. I wasn't hungry. Anxiety bounced in my belly. I ordered a double espresso and, when my waiter left, I lifted my chin to the sun and closed my eyes. I saw color, then the shape of a god's eye, a design woven out of yarn onto a wooden cross. I saw Adèle sitting at a picnic table beside the Garonne River in Auvillar, sketching. I remembered her identity photo, her lips in a pout, her angry eyes glaring. I saw her behind the barbed-wire fence at Septfonds. I opened my eyes and glanced at a couple sitting nearby, their heads bent in conversation. I wanted to ask them what they knew of Septfonds. "Septfonds?" they would ask. And if they knew Septfonds at all, they would tell me it was the name of a charming village not far from here.

"And the internment camp?" I would ask.

I assumed they would not know.

On Saturday morning, I pored over my tourist map and looked for a symbol that designated a synagogue. Nothing. Inside the tourist bureau, a woman had marked my map. I walked along Quai Montmurat and looked for rue Saint Claire. Quai Montmurat turned into Quai de Verdun. I turned right and passed an office building, a parking lot, and nondescript apartment buildings. No synagogue. I noticed a man and woman standing and talking outside their cars. "*Pardon.*" Both turned. "*Un question, s'il vous plaît. Une synagogue. Près d'ici?*"

The man repeated: "*Synagogue, synagogue.*"

The word was nearly the same in French and English. What didn't he understand? "*Synagogue de les juifs.*"

"No, no *synagogue.*"

He understood *les juifs*, and I knew instantly that this word had closed our conversation. Still, I persisted. "Temple."

"Ah," the woman said, her face brightening. "*Je vous prendrai.*" She would take me.

Together we walked back the way I'd come, turning left at the corner. We entered a building, then an office where a slight, balding man rounded a desk. Yes, yes, he spoke English. My escort left. The man would be delighted to show me the temple. And I, too, was delighted to have found what I was looking for.

I followed along a corridor. "*Temple juif,*" I said.

He stopped abruptly. "Ah no, this is a Protestant temple."

We walked back along Rue Saint Claire, past the parking lot where I'd chatted with the man and woman. Then he stopped. The next building was the synagogue. The façade was austere, flush with the sidewalk and rising at a sharp angle. There was no courtyard, no approach. The building had three doors, the center door protected by an iron grate. My escort rang a bell and, when no one answered, he shrugged and fidgeted. Obviously, he was eager to leave. I thanked him and said I'd linger a while.

I crossed the street to get a better view. On the second floor were two stained-glass windows with geometric shapes, no six-pointed Star of David, no menorah, nothing to mark this as a Jewish house of worship. The stained glass was so dark I could not imagine light filtering through. It was as if this building wore camouflage.

I crossed again and searched each doorway for a *meẓuẓah*, a small case with a parchment scroll that Jews nailed at an angle to the doorposts. The writing on a scroll inside was the *shema*, a Hebrew prayer that commanded us to keep God's words in our minds and our hearts.

No *meẓuẓah*.

Once again, I crossed the street and, because I wanted a wider view in my camera lens, backed myself against a building. Beside me, a wooden shutter flew open and a dark-haired woman, maybe in her mid-thirties, eyed me warily. I nearly chirped, "Bonjour, Madame. Do you speak English?"

She assessed me and, seeing an old woman obviously American, her face softened. "A little," she said.

"The synagogue. Do people come here?"

"They come when they have something to celebrate."

"I was hoping to see someone." Saturday morning was a time of worship.

"I think a few hours ago someone came. I think, earlier, when I looked out, the door was open. Now, it is closed."

"They have gone?"

"*Oui*. They have gone."

I felt as if we were discussing an exotic species nearing extinction.

I walked back to the center of Montauban and stopped for an espresso before wandering. Bells in a steeple rang. I followed a random street and found myself in a neighborhood of Sixties-style cement buildings. No gardens. No lawns. A few bars. A few cafés. I passed them all. I'd missed lunch. Was I hollowing out my belly in sympathy with Adèle's empty belly? She was so much on my mind.

And then I saw them, vertical banners announcing *Lycée Michelet*.

Adèle's school. How strange that fate had brought me here. An iron fence surrounded a large lawn, but even from this distance I was able to read the carved letters: *lycée des jeunes filles*. School for young girls.

I tried the gate. Locked.

At the *Lycée Michelet*, Adèle was a girl among girls, carrying her books, talking with friends, walking home to eat supper with her mother and father. She was seventeen when she moved with her family to Auvillar. I vividly remembered my seventeenth summer. I was a recent high school graduate, so full of life I bubbled with effervescence. I was in love with my high school sweetheart. Those were the days when I believed I wouldn't go to college. I'd realized my dream of dancing with the Rockettes on the stage of Radio City Music Hall in New York City. I spent my time between shows lounging on the grass in Central Park. I chose to leave that life behind for another. I'd had that choice.

I thought of Anne Frank. Mostly or maybe especially if we were American and we considered the *Shoah*, we latched on to the story of Anne Frank. One line particularly catches our attention, Anne Frank declaring that we are all good at heart. Repeating that thought we assuage our guilt and our culpability, for ours is a world without justice and this is the real lesson of Anne Frank's diary and of Adèle Kurzweil's life — that we are not just, not kind, not fair, and not all good at heart. Auschwitz is proof of that. Who knew to what depths Anne fell in Bergen-Belsen where she died? Adèle had gotten it right with her sideways glare, her pout, and her defiance.

I followed my map and searched for the *Musée de la Résistance et de la Déportation,* another site in Odile's home city that she knew nothing about until I said I would be visiting it. I entered a park and walked paths, passing an Olympic-size swimming pool. I passed clumps of students milling about, smoking, sitting on the grass, listening to music. A sign on a low building announced a recreation center. Where was the museum? Maybe someone inside would give me directions.

I peered into an office. A woman looked up from her desk. Yes, the museum was here. If I left her office, turned right, and walked to the end of the corridor, I would see the museum on my left.

The first thing I saw was an eight-foot cardboard cutout of Hitler, arm raised in a Nazi salute. *Okay, I get it. He is the villain — not us, not the French.*

I entered a large room that looked more like a warehouse than a museum — stark white walls, high ceilings and track lights. I felt disoriented. No map, no diagram, no guard or friendly volunteer to ask for assistance. Like Septfonds, this place was unattended, and I was the sole visitor.

Photographs, maps, and artifacts assaulted me. Where to begin? Finally, I figured out that these exhibits were a history of war, the First World War, the Second World War, the Cold War, the French war in Algeria. Despite its title, *Musée de la Résistance et de la Déportation*, this was not a museum specific to Vichy France, collaboration, resistance, and Jews.

Because of Gerhard, I knew the Kurzweil suitcases were here on display, along with Adèle's drawings. I passed cases with guns and uniforms. I passed military campaign maps. I realized I was moving through a history of French wars. I stood in front of a large map marking France's internment camps and found Septfonds. I wound my way among displays, wartime ration tickets, a photograph of Marshal Pétain visiting Montaubaun, crowds greeting him. Then, there they were — the Kurzweil suitcases and artifacts, carelessly displayed in a back corner as if they were an afterthought. I remembered Gerhard saying that Pascal Caïla had removed some of the Kurzweil belongings and stored them in his mother's attic for safekeeping. I hadn't understood why someone would remove precious items from a museum. Wasn't a museum a place of preservation? Now, I understood.

Here on tables were Adèle's fashion sketches, her books, her identity card with her pouting sullen face. I looked down at her sketch of a woman, her face in profile, her long hair curling. She had initialed the drawing in her own hand, a scrolling A and a scrolling K back to back. Her diary sat open on a table. I translated. "Tomorrow is the end of the school year. I am sad to leave my friends, but happy to spend more time with my parents in the lovely village of Auvillar."

I could have torn that page, kept that page, taken the entire diary and her sketches. No one would have seen, noticed, or cared. Even now, no one protected her.

19

L ate one afternoon in Paris, I accepted a ride with two strangers. As I crossed a street, guidebook in hand, I noticed a sturdy-look-ing, dark-haired man, standing behind a car parked at a corner, and smoking a cigarette. I needed directions, so I approached him. He held up a hand, signaling me to wait as he walked to the passenger's window and knocked on the glass. The window slid down. A woman with dark hair and dark eyes stuck her head out and turned toward me as if to say, who are you? What do you want? Like the man, she was probably in her mid-thirties. They spoke. She opened the door, took out her iPhone, then motioned to my guidebook, which was still in the man's hands. She entered the name of the street I'd written, *rue du Bac*. "Ooh la," she said.

She sat with her legs outside the car. I leaned over and read the screen on her iPhone. Twenty-five minutes away. "To walk or to ride?" I asked.

"To walk, yes. You must take the bus instead," she said.

I understood. She was telling me I could not walk because it was too far. I must take a bus. But, I was a walker. "I will be fine," I said.

Both spoke in rapid French. I believe he was the one who suggested driving me, although she, the English speaker, voiced the suggestion.

"Oh, no," I said. "I can't do that."

"We will take you," she said.

I shook my head and waved my index finger like a metronome. My errand was frivolous. I was tracking down a shop where I'd once bought wild, unique patterned stockings.

"I am...," she paused. "How shall I say? No problem."

Safe, she meant. "It's not that," I said quickly. Although it *was* that. How could I, a woman of a certain age, schooled against taking rides with strangers, get in that car? Yet, that's exactly what I did, climbed into the back seat as the woman set her phone, now a GPS, onto the dash. The man tossed his cigarette away, and we were off, driving through the maze of streets in Saint Germaine des Près, the woman practicing her English, me practicing my French, both of us thoroughly enjoying each other's company. I had no idea what made me get in that car. I was, as the French say, *en ce moment*. Call it luck, karma, serendipity, or perhaps one person doing a favor for another, but there I was, happily riding in a car with strangers. Wasn't that what travel was about, finding that essential part of yourself that connected you to others?

It was the hour when work ended and evening began. People sat at tables outside cafés, sipping beer, coffee or wine. Inside the car we exchanged stories, where I lived, if I had children. The man was from Portugal, the woman from Brazil. She had a first cousin in Los Angeles. She planned to visit England, but her English was not so good anymore. I told her that in England, her English would return.

We pulled up in front of number 77 rue du Bac. I offered a five-euro bill. Both refused. I thanked them.

When I visited Germaine the next day, she said, "You are like me. You are lucky." We did have luck, Germaine and I, and something more — an innate or a learned toughness — and, although we were older, Germaine two decades older than I, each of us continued to feel the thrill of possibility.

Germaine's table was set with the blue-and-yellow provincial print placemats I remembered from earlier visits, the same white plates, the same silverware. I loved the comfortable intimacy of this flat. Germaine had prepared her signature dish, meaty croquettes, and, once again, I — who was now a pescatarian — quietly ate meat without protest along with rice and an endive salad dressed simply with olive oil, lemon juice, salt and pepper. There was the requisite baguette and a carafe of red wine. We were four at the table, Valerie, Aline, Germaine, and I.

Germaine fingered the strap of her watch and turned it. "A journalist came," she said.

"Recently?" I said. Time was difficult in translation. Near past? Distant past?

"Maybe a week now," Aline said. "She was making a documentary about French Judaism and French anti-Semitism. She came to interview my mother."

I felt a tug in my belly. Unlike me, this journalist was the real thing.

"I cannot bear anti-Semitism," Germaine said. "My father's sister and her son were deported."

This was both an old and a new story. I knew about the deportation of her father's sister, but not about the boy. I thought of Germaine's father, her mother, and four of her sisters living out the war years in their posh flat near the *Arc de Triomphe*. Had Nissim Rousso had contact with his sister? Had he known of her deportation? How old was the boy? Why did no one hide him? He survived. His mother did not.

Aline paused, knife midair. "Growing up, I knew my cousin had been deported, but I didn't know what that meant."

Germaine pulled herself up to the table and held fast to her story. "I did not want them to know. I did not want them to carry this burden."

I listened to sounds of forks coming to rest on plates. I thought of Aline wandering the flat in the Thirteenth Arrondissement and discovering those photos of the concentration camps in Léon's books. She hadn't connected her great-aunt and her cousin to those photos. No one had told her. Yet, for Germaine, the *Shoah* was a benchmark. Léon's work, his histories of anti-Semitism and of persecutions, she had said on another occasion, gave her an understanding of where she came from. She felt connected to a Jewish community. Léon was secular; and he was also fiercely Jewish. She understood she could connect to her past without God. Without ritual.

She sat back in her chair. "I am very sad for the sinking boats, for the people," she said, referring to the stories of tragic deaths of the refugees in the Mediterranean that were so prevalent in the news.

"French people are afraid they are going to eat our bread," Aline said.

Wasn't that the cry during the Second World War, not enough food, not enough bread? As was her style, Germaine did not linger on the sadness of our times, and perhaps this was what had allowed her to survive and to thrive. She felt sadness and moved on. "I am ashamed to say this, but this is the truth. During the war, I was happy."

I understood. She was young and in love with Ralph, her handsome charismatic prince. He was eighteen when they met; she was twenty-one. All the girls wanted Ralph, and he chose Germaine. Wartime heightens our senses. None of the usual rules and customs of family or class apply. Germaine was free to love her prince. Then, quickly, perhaps too quickly, she became a mother. Yet, somehow, Germaine had managed to care first for one infant, then another, and also to care for girls in *la colonie*. Madame Gordin had mothered her and Germaine had belonged to a community. Still, she must have known unhappiness, Ralph's infidelities, her parents' absence. The nature of perception and of memory is to see and not see, to remember and not remember. Such uncertainty is disorienting, so we construct certainty out of perception. This, I supposed, was Germaine's story: she was truly happy.

What story do I construct? I have never told the story I am telling now of packing a suitcase and driving into the dark, a lone car on a deserted country road. Dick and I had argued. The boys were asleep in their beds. Dick had watched me throw clothes into a suitcase. Why didn't he stop me? I wanted him to stop me. No way could I stop myself. Too often, I found my life as wife and mother miserable and exhausting. My mother had hooked herself to my father's demands and whims, something I had refused to do with my husband. Driving, I looked through the windshield and saw myself floating above the trees and above the life I'd created, a figure in a Chagall painting. I wasn't real — not to myself. I liked that feeling of floating, my headlights making a tunnel I passed through. But where was I going? Where would I spend the night? At a motel? Slowly, the rumble of the car's engine mixing with the sifting sounds of the tires eased my tension, but not my worry. The floating figure descended. My skin absorbed her. I loved my children. I loved my husband. This was my life. I had to make my way inside this marriage. I stopped at a phone booth and called home. Tears streamed.

"Come home," Dick said. "Just come home."

Aline and Valerie cleared the table. Aline carried her mother's apple tart from the kitchen. Germaine tasted and nodded; the tart met a standard she had set for herself. She spoke of Aline's and Stanley's marriage, the two of them standing under a *huppah*. Shortly after, she and Léon were married in a religious ceremony. The year was 1972. A rabbi performed the ceremony in his study. No one attended. Germaine did not believe they needed a religious ceremony. She did this for her husband. "For Léon, it was important that our marriage be accepted in Israel, too," Germaine said.

I imagined that, for a man who had seen what Léon had seen, a safe harbor, no matter how mythical, was a necessity. Unlike Germaine, Aline and her sister observed Jewish holidays, and on those days Germaine prepared traditional dishes. Her flat was the place where the family gathered. Aline's son, the only one of Germaine's grandchildren to become a bar mitzvah, read the prayers in Hebrew.

"I was happy to do that, prepare this food," Germaine said.

"This is what she likes to do," Aline said.

Before Passover, I cooked for days, making matzoh ball soup; a first-cut brisket or a chicken dish; and *tsimis*, a mixture of carrots, sweet potatoes and turnips that Mama used to make. I grated a horseradish root. Some of my family was Jewish; others were not. All were welcome at my table, family and friends. On Passover, my family arrived from Colorado, New York City, and Vermont. Old friends drove in from New Hampshire. We gathered in the kitchen, spilled into the living room, and moved to the dining room.

"Next Sunday she will cook for fourteen," Aline said. "We will put a long table here in the living room." Aline said. "It is my birthday."

Germaine offered her plate. "*Plus petit,*" she said to Aline, asking for a second but smaller wedge of tart. She took a bite and spoke to me of her hundredth birthday. She was ninety-seven and planning ahead. I hoped this was her destiny. "Will you come?"

I lowered my fork. "I will come, and I will bring roses." *A hundred roses*, I vowed silently. Then I wondered how in the world I'd wrap my arms around a hundred roses. Like Germaine, I would manage.

20

"Do you see?" he asked.

I did not see.

I'd joined this walking tour to see a side of the Marais unfamiliar to me, but why were we stopping here? I saw nothing remarkable about the architecture, no beautiful old columns or friezes, no striking contemporary steel and glass. Brian, our guide, had walked up to a limestone building block and traced something with his finger. Nearly all of Paris was constructed of limestone dug from deposits that dated from a time when France was once an inland sea.

Brian traced the shape again for my benefit.

I stepped closer. An impression. The imprint of a spiral shell, a remnant of a creature that had lived millions and millions of years ago. Sediment had formed and encased the shell. Eventually the shell had cracked and dissolved, leaving an impression that dated from the Mesozoic Era, a time that ended with the extinction of dinosaurs. Like most children, I'd had a fascination with dinosaurs, looking up, up, up at the skeletons in the Museum of Natural History in New York City. Now I tried to get my head around the idea of dinosaurs roaming here in

Paris. I ran the pad of my index finger over the indentation. Did all limestone building blocks hold remnants of a past that stretched back to a time before human evolution?

My purse weighed heavily on my shoulder. Always, I carried too much: iPad, phone, journal, water bottle, sweater, and an umbrella just in case. Brian had stopped on a narrow sidewalk while the group waited for access to a courtyard. Inside an iron gate, a guard house. This was the courtyard of the Hôtel de Beauvais, a building shaped and constructed to accommodate the asymmetry of the land. It was a masterpiece of seventeenth-century architecture with its balcony, columns, and undulating horseshoe façade.

This was not a place where you rented a room and stayed for a night or a weekend. This was a *hôtel particulier*, a mansion where nobility had lived, and this one had belonged to Catherine de Beauvais — favored because, according to legend, she was the first lover of a very young Louis XIV. In French, *hôtel* translates as both inn and looking after. *Particulier* means private or personal. In a *hôtel particulier*, servants did the looking after, Brian said, reminding us of France's heritage of kings and queens, of royal plots and royal privilege, and of the wreckage they left behind.

Ordinary houses in the Marais shared walls. A *hôtel particulier* stood free and had both an impressive entrance court and a garden. I loved gardens and I wanted to see the one of the Hôtel de Beauvais but it was hidden in an inner courtyard to which we did not have access. The building was now home to the Administrative Court of Appeals of Paris, so here we were, visiting a public place closed to the public.

I marveled at the columns and architectural details, their names tucked into an inaccessible fold of my brain. Which columns were Corinthian? Which were Doric? Brian spoke of a keystone, and memory surfaced indistinctly. Something about equal distribution of weight. Ah yes, the final piece, inserted to support tons and tons of stone. Here, each keystone featured a carved head. Brian pointed to a homely female face with bulging eyes, thick lips, and hair like the Medusa. This was Catherine de Beauvais, and I wondered if I were looking at an artist's joke or verisimilitude.

We made our way back along the rue François Miron, passing the limestone block where I'd traced the imprint of the spiral shell. I didn't see it, but I knew it was there. Wasn't this what most of us wanted in life, to leave our mark? If not an imprint, then a story?

The group entered the *allée des Justes*, Passage of the Just, outside the *Mémorial de la Shoah*. Here a wall of brass plaques honored French men and women named Righteous among the Nations, non-Jews who had risked their lives to save Jews during the German Occupation. I thought of Adriènne Laquièze driving the girls who had lived in *la colonie*, but I did not have time to search for her name.

The group gathered at a forest-green sculpture. "A Wallace Fountain," Brian said. I'd visited this plaza countless times and passed by without seeing. Whatever that said about me, it wasn't good. Brian explained that during the Franco-Prussian War of 1870-71, when fighting had nearly destroyed Paris's water supply, Sir Richard Wallace designed these fountains and had them installed throughout the city. Four caryatids: Kindness, Simplicity, Charity, and Sobriety supported a pointed dome where water trickled — good, clean drinking water flowing since the middle of the nineteenth century.

I filled my empty water bottle, wondering again at my blindness to these caryatids and this continuous flow of fresh water.

At the end of our passageway, four policemen, dressed in blue and carrying assault rifles, stood outside a black van. To their right, three soldiers wearing camouflage stood on the steps to the *Mémorial de la Shoah*, weapons at the ready. Brian gathered the group. "This is not a tour of Jewish history, but I cannot pass this spot. I must speak," he said. "Vichy collaborated with the Nazis and France deported seventy-five thousand Jews, including eleven thousand children. The Nazis were not interested in the children, but Vichy did not want all those Jewish orphans."

His voice caught at the back of his throat, and he gave a little cough. The shock of those deported children stilled the group. My throat tightened.

The light changed, and we crossed *rue Geoffroy-l'Asnier*. Now a quick right, then a left. A narrow passage ended in a T. To my left, an alcove with a broken sculpture of a woman and beneath her form, cigarette butts, candy wrappers, and the smell of urine. We had gone only a few steps before Brian paused before an iron fence. Behind it, an ordinary stucco apartment building — no signature moldings, no iron balconies, no details to mark time. In this alley, buildings and trees blocked the light. A dusty vine climbed one wall and the entire place — alley, yard, building — had the feel of abandonment and neglect.

Brian pointed out a box about two feet high, fashioned to resemble a house. On my own I would have missed it. A plaque with portraits and names had been fastened to one side: Elijas the father, Sarah the mother, their three sons. All rounded up, deported, murdered. "A fourth child, not pictured, returned from deportation and the camps to commemorate her mother, her father, and her brothers," Brian said.

I wondered about Brian's connection to these events. Did he have a personal history, relatives lost? You don't need a personal connection to feel the horror, the injustice, and the cruelty. You need empathy. I was grateful to Brian for taking us down this alley and showing us preserved memory here among dust, grit, and curling leaves.

He opened a low gate. In Paris, I had a sense of locking out and locking in, so many wooden doors and iron gates concealing or protecting. This was *l'Hôtel de Sens*, another *hôtel particulier*, this one on *rue du Figuier*, originally owned by Tristan de Salazar, Archbishop of Sens. Brian looked down into the gravel at our feet. I looked, too, thinking he'd dropped a coin or a key. "Limestone," he said, still looking. He stooped down, plucked something up, and dropped a tiny spiral shell into my open palm.

In my hotel room, I transferred the spiral shell to the coin compartment of my wallet where I carried euros, quarters, dimes and pennies. This was my last night in Paris for a while, my last night in France, and I felt the rhythm of a stay that was ending. I was melancholy but not sad; alone but not lonely. I touched the shell. Paris remembered and that was good.

At Charles De Gaulle Airport, an official looked down at my passport photo, then up at my face. I willed calm into my skin and resisted the urge to shift my weight from foot to foot. Always at passport control, I was aware of my middle name: Hirsch. Crazy. You're being paranoid, I told myself. No one waited for me in the shadows. No one had my name on a list. I could not stop thinking about those deported children. Had I been living in Paris that summer of 1942 I could have — no, likely would have — been one of those eleven thousand. How easily our stories could have been reversed. Specificity mattered — where we'd been born, where we lived, and at what time in history. The color of our skin mattered. Religion mattered. The customs officer picked up a stamp and brought it down hard on my passport. I made my way to my gate. Standing in line on the jet-way, I adjusted the straps of my backpack and peered around shoulders to see if folks in line ahead of me were moving. At the plane's door, I looked into the cockpit at a pilot's lined face. I was not at peace. Something felt unfinished. I was searching. What for? What was missing? I fingered the spiral shell in my pocket as if to find my answer. I took my seat, buckled up and sat back ready for takeoff.

EPILOGUE
Shehecheyanu

The last of the sun's rays streamed through the glass of the sliding doors and illuminated my guests, forty loved friends and family, all sitting in metal folding chairs, all facing the sun, the brick patio and a hedge of sea roses. Because of the sun's brilliance there would be no photographs. Later, this struck me as fitting. Traditionally, Jews do not allow photographers into a sanctuary. Our bodies would hold memory in flesh and bone.

Here in my home at the edge of the sea, colors and sounds were ever-changing. This was where the family had gathered to remember my mother and to cast her ashes, where five years later, we cast my father's ashes, Rabbi Lev facilitating both services. I felt my parents' presence, as if they were here in this room, my mother radiating warmth and support, my father wearing a look of proud skepticism and saying, "A bat mitzvah at your age? What're you, nuts?" Then, he'd laugh his infectious laugh.

Because Lev had recently moved to Austin, Texas, Sue, his dear friend and mine, was leading my service. Dark-haired, full-bodied and exuberant with life, Sue was genuinely and completely who she was — Jew, woman, wife, mother, singer, teacher, friend. Not an ounce of artifice in her body. She reminded me of the women of my childhood, Mama, my Aunt Ida, Mrs. Botkin, and Mrs. Klein, who openly shared the intensity of their lives.

I wore a print silk dress, the colors of the sea, turquoise, pale blue, deep blue, a little green. Raina, my oldest grandchild, wore a flowing cream-colored dress, and she'd done up her hair in a French twist. She placed my *tallit* over my shoulders, and as she ran her fingers along the edges, I felt the ancestral touch of my people. Traditionally, the older generation passed the Torah down to the next generation, and that was what we had done at Raina's bat mitzvah two weeks earlier in Denver, standing on the *bima* of her synagogue. Today our roles had reversed, and it was my grand-daughter who passed the Torah up through time to me. Raina was sixteen, a late bat mitzvah, and if she was late, what was I? But what did age matter? At that moment, time past melted into time present.

My three granddaughters and I stood before our guests, Nina wearing white lace with pointy-toed, high-heeled beige pumps, Lilly choosing a sheer dark blue flowered dress with a teal under-slip. Zeke, my grandson, not one to stand before a crowd, was present, but not here on our improvised *bima*. Dick sat in the front row. My sons and my two daughers-in-law sat among my friends. I fingered the border of my *tallit* embroidered in white with Hebrew letters, white on white, heat on heat. Odile had shown me Hebrew letters she'd formed from clay. I thought of Daniel speaking of his belief in oneness, a feeling that transcended time. Was that God?

Never before this moment had I worn a *tallit*, and I felt the love and weight of centuries inextricably woven into each thread. Here were music and prayers, Yiddish and Hebrew. Here was the fruity scent of

Passover wine, the taste of hope mingled with the taste of grief. The fragility and the strength of my people rested on my shoulders, and now I understood why Ernst Bohrmann had run into a burning synagogue on Kristallnacht to rescue the *tallit*.

This was my *shehecheyanu* moment, the *shehecheyanu*, my favorite prayer, celebrating what was new or what felt new, like a hike in my beloved White Mountains, Raina's bat mitzvah, my bat mitzvah. To prepare, I had carried a transliteration of the *shehecheyanu* in my pocket and sung out loud as I hiked solo to summits with my dogs.

Observant Jews whispered the *shehecheyanu* when they tasted the first peach of the season or the first ripe plum, blending the tastes of a summer that had passed with one just newly arriving. I conjured Mama, her mandelbrot, her chicken soup, her *tsimis*, her warm freshly churned applesauce. These were the tastes and scents inside the yellow stucco house where Mama's hands circled flames, then came to rest in front of her eyes as she welcomed *shabbos* into our lives.

Because I loved the *havdalah* service, my bat mitzvah took place on a Saturday evening. *Havdalah* lifts us from the sanctity of *shabbat* and places us gently into the week ahead. I remembered standing as a young girl on the front porch and watching for the first three stars to appear in the sky, first on Friday night to welcome *shabbos*, then on Saturday to signal its end. Both times, I would race into the house to tell Mama: it's starting; it's over.

For the *havdalah* service, you needed a braided candle, a cup of wine and fragrant spices. That afternoon, Raina, Nina, Lilly, my grandson Zeke, and I had filled small net bags with cloves, cinnamon sticks and nutmeg. We stood around the kitchen counter, and I thought of the spiral shell I'd slipped into my pocket. Since my return from France, it had become a talisman for me.

Now, as Sue strummed the notes of a wordless melody on her guitar, Zeke hauled back and hurled spice bags to each of my guests. Zeke's mom sat, stiff-backed, eyes looking beyond her son. Generally, I wasn't easy going when Zeke acted out, and she knew this, but tonight, I could honestly say, I didn't mind his rambunctiousness. A gangly ten-year-old, all weekend long, he had been trying to find his place or just a little space among my gregarious, outgoing granddaughters,

He was growing like a weed, and his black trousers hung only to his ankle bones. He wore a white dress shirt, a red bow tie and massive sneakers because he'd refused his dress shoes, claiming they were too tight.

I held a spice bag to my nose and breathed the final scents of *shabbat*, cinnamon, cloves, and nutmeg, symbolizing rest, contemplation, love and life. I wished Germaine were here, Germaine who had said over and over she didn't believe in ritual, didn't like ritual. I think she would have liked these rituals, words, scents and the notes of Sue's guitar lifting us all into a place where spirit dwelled.

Sue's vibrant soprano voice filled my heart as she sang the blessings, first over wine, then spices. Nina lit the three wicks of the braided *havdalah* candle, and we thanked God — the God I did and didn't believe in — for the gift of fire. We sang the blessing for *havdalah* itself, that separation of sacred and secular, of light and dark. I took the candle from Nina's hand and drowned the flame in wine.

Each of my guests had a printed program and a song sheet along with transliterations. We sang *Eliyahu HaNavi*, Elijah the Prophet, joy swelling inside this room. I felt as if I were riding a current that flowed through generations, then floating above my granddaughters' voices, each beautiful, each vibrant. Zeke did not sing, but he joined us on the *bima*, and I rested a hand on his shoulder.

As with most Hebrew prayers, the *Shehecheyanu* has many meanings, and now as we sang, we honored those who gave us life — parents, grandparents, and great grandparents, Jews and non-Jews in this room, reaching back to distant shores where our ancestors traveled from known or unknown villages into this new world. *Baruch Attah Adoni Eloheinu melach ha olam, shehecheyanu, vikimanu, vihigyanu, lazman, hazeh.* Blessed are You, Adoni, for giving us life, for sustaining us and allowing us to reach this joyous moment in time. So many sustained us, family, friends, children, grandchildren. In Yiddish, our extended families are our *machatunim.* I loved that, a name for this extension that brings us together. I claimed it all, my *machatunim,* my spiritual tradition, my biblical tradition, secular knowledge and my people's history and culture.

Raina escorted me to a chair, and I sat facing Sue and my three granddaughters. The girls had a surprise for me, a song they'd practiced and memorized, "Home" by Phillip Phillips, and I felt as if I were closing a circle, becoming a daughter of the covenant on my own terms, my granddaughters, my grandson, all of my family and my friends, filling this room with joy and love as the girls sang, "… I'm gonna make this place your home."

The service ended. I rose from my chair and waited as each of my guests filed up the stairs to rooms above where a caterer had worked his magic. On a dining room wall, Germaine's framed collage faced east to the horizon. I stepped outside, stood on the deck and looked up at the stars. The sea shifted. I was a Jew, a daughter of the covenant — a pinprick of light in the night sky.

Afterword

When *The Spiral Shell* launched in April of 2020, I was sheltering in place. The country was in lockdown, everywhere the news showed images of the dying and the dead, and aired soundbites of nurses and doctors pleading for protective gear, while refrigerator trucks in our cities parked outside of hospitals to await the arrival of more corpses. Those not afflicted with the virus hunkered down as the pandemic raged through meat-packing plants, targeting the poor, the undocumented, and people of color, who were already struggling on the edge of survival.

Given this unfolding global nightmare, a new book seemed inconsequential. Yet, *The Spiral Shell* was due out that spring, on April 20th, just two months after the official lockdown due to the Covid-19 pandemic. I was eighty-one and this was my debut memoir.

In early February of 2020, I signed up for a workshop called "Demystifying Social Media," I had no idea that within six weeks all of my previously scheduled in-person book events would have to be cancelled; nor did I know that through this workshop I would meet and befriend my instructor, the novelist and memoirist Jenna Blum, who would soon become my fairy godmother and wave her magic wand over *The Spiral Shell*.

Coincidentally, Jenna and novelist Caroline Leavitt, had just founded "A Mighty Blaze", a Facebook site dedicated to writers who were bringing out books during Covid, and selected my book as one the featured titles for promotion.

As a guest on "A Mighty Blaze"; I attended "Blaze" events, and learned to do my own Zoom appearances at libraries and book stores. At one of those events, I met novelist L. Annette Binder, author of *The Vanishing Sky*. Both of us had written World War II stories about ordinary people surviving in extraordinary times. We may have seemed an unlikely pairing, a novelist writing from a German point of view, a memoirist writing from a Jewish point of view, a younger woman, an older woman, but we shared remarkably similar sensibilities about war and the effects of war on daily life. Annette and I showed slides. We read passages from our books, particularly about women and mothers who had persevered. I read about Germaine Poliakov, who as a young woman had cared for Jewish refugee children in a secret house in the south of France during the Nazi occupation and somehow the themes of resilience, endurance, and just plain luck seemed all the more relevant to my readers and audience now.

I described Germaine pregnant and running across a field, carrying her baby in one arm as she dragged her toddler with another while bullets sprayed the air. And, I spoke of Germaine on my last visit to her apartment in Paris in October 2019, eight years since our first meeting. Her daughter Aline, the baby in Germaine's arms that day in 1942, met me on the landing outside her mother's flat. I was carrying an advanced reading copy (arc) of *The Spiral Shell*. Aline offered her cheeks, and we kiss kissed, the French way. "She is much changed," Aline said. "She walks with a walker. She is bent over. Her knees do not straighten. She does not remember. She may not know who you are."

Sitting in one of the upholstered apricot velvet French provincial chairs in her living room, Germaine looked up as I entered. "Ah, Sandell."

That day, Germaine insisted I sign the advance copy, and when I handed it back, she held it to her heart. In December that year she celebrated her one hundred and first birthday. Then, one morning the following February she passed away, just weeks before the arrival of Covid in our lives, as well as the publication of this book.

Germaine was passionate about life. She baked apple tarts into her nineties. She told me her story, and I am telling her story to you, along with the stories of others. Stories link us to both our past and future. Stories linger long after the book has closed.

Acknowledgments

I am grateful to my readers, Judy Bolton-Fasman, Jan Clausen, Kristen Cosby and Katherine Towler; to Marilyn Kallet who sent me a name; to my Fellow Fellows at the Virginia Center for the Creative Arts for their wisdom and encouragement, to Victoria Simon and Sue Gold for their steadfast friendship throughout this process; to Valerie Fert for her friendship, translations, and gifts of time; to Germaine Poliakov, Yvonne Lieser, Robert Losson, and Gerhard Schneider for sharing their stories; to Wildacres Retreat for my cabin in the woods; and to the Virginia Center for the Creative Arts in Virginia and in France for quiet spaces where the work flowed.